GETTING STARTED IN CREATIVE REAL ESTATE INVESTING

By E. Wright Davis, JD

Copyright © E. Wright Davis 2011

Copyright

Waiver of Legal Liability

Getting Started in Creative Real Estate Investing

Table of contents

Table of Contents... continued

Table of Contents... continued

Acknowledgements

I wish to express my deepest gratitude to the following people who helped make this book possible:

To Gail White of Tailored PC Documents, to whom I am greatly appreciative for her word processing, organizational and publishing skills. (www.tailoredpcdocuments.biz)

And to my wife, Cynthia, whose talent and computer skills made this book come together.

And my students who have taken my investing courses, Mega Mortgages, Cracking the Mortgage Code, Calculator Power, Getting Started in Creative Real Estate Investing, and my students in the real estate salesman and mortgage broker licensing courses throughout the years who gave me the inspiration and ideas for this book.

www.realestateinvesting.ewrightdavis.com

About the Author

E. Wright Davis

A member of the State Bar of Georgia for more than forty years, mortgage broker, real estate investor, realtor and title insurance company president.

The author and creator of five real estate investment courses and has developed an online real estate law course for a major university.

As a state supreme court certified mediator in two states, he understands real estate dispute resolution and foreclosure resolution.

Is the author of four books; *Legal Vengeance* (fiction), *Mega Mortgages* and *How to Crack the Mortgage Code,* and *Getting Started in Creative Real Estate Investing.*

For ten years he was a state licensed real estate salesperson and real estate broker instructor.

Served as a U.S. Delegate to the U.S.–China Conference on Trade Investment and Economic Law in Beijing China and was selected as One of Five Outstanding Men of Georgia by the Georgia Jaycees.

www.realestateinvesting.ewrightdavis.com

Cash to existing mortgage offer

There are many situations in which it is advantageous for an investor to use cash to purchase a property.

Sellers who have to act quickly appreciate a simple offer, even if the offer does not offer a lot of cash. For example, a seller facing foreclosure will not want to become involved in a complicated drawn out closing.

Everyone wants to know how much they are going to receive and when. This type of offer is simple and easy to explain.

Offer

Before

After

LARGE EQUITY → CASH FOR ALL OR PART OF EQUITY →

EXISTING FIRST → PURCHASER TAKES SUBJECT TO →

EQUITY EQUAL TO DIFFERENCE BETWEEN FIRST AND MARKET VALUE

SOLVE FIRST

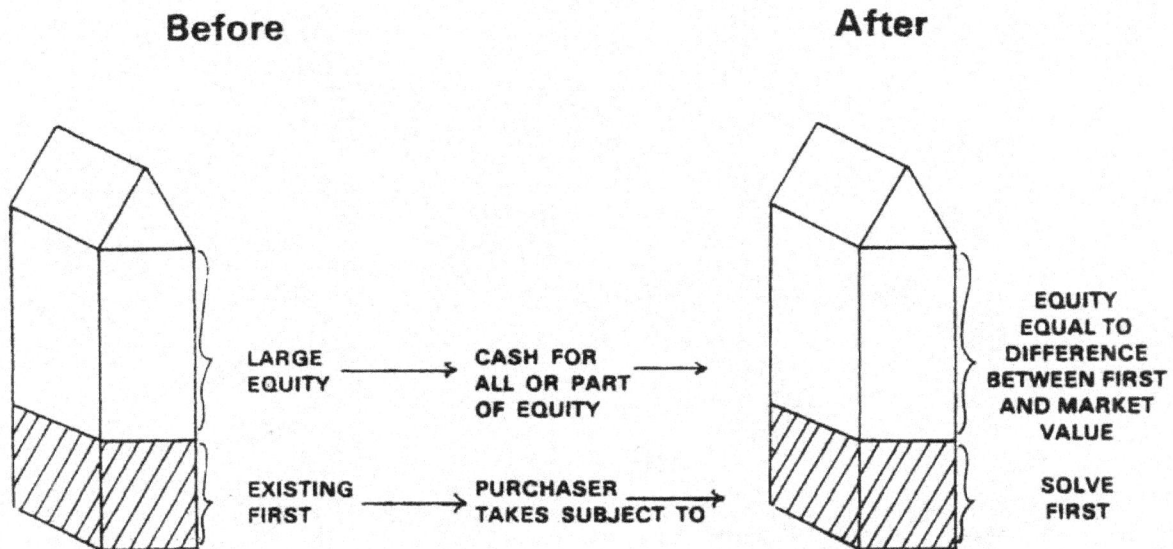

This is the simplest creative real estate technique. You offer cash for all or part of the equity, and purchase the property "subject to" the existing debt.

You do not want to "assume" the debt, because you are then liable in the event of default. Your offer should state: "_____ dollars down, and take title subject to the existing indebtedness to _____".

Benefits

To the Purchaser	To the Seller
1. Purchaser can act fast to acquire bargain.	1. Seller receives fast action
2. Existing loan can be taken intact – great for low interest rate loans.	2. No confusion over complicated closing or terms.
3. Purchaser can re-coup down payment by getting a second after closing.	3. Minimal closing costs for buyer or seller.
	4. Property is sold!

Notes:

_____

_____

_____

_____

_____

_____

_____

Cash to existing mortgage with seller carry-back financing

Like offer number one, this offer gives the seller cash in a fast not so complicated way. This offer is useful in many of the same situations as the previous offer.

The major difference here is that the seller, in addition to the cash, receives a note for a portion of his equity. This note is secured against the subject property with a mortgage (in some states Deeds of Trust are used instead of mortgages). Again, the buyer takes the existing debt "subject to."

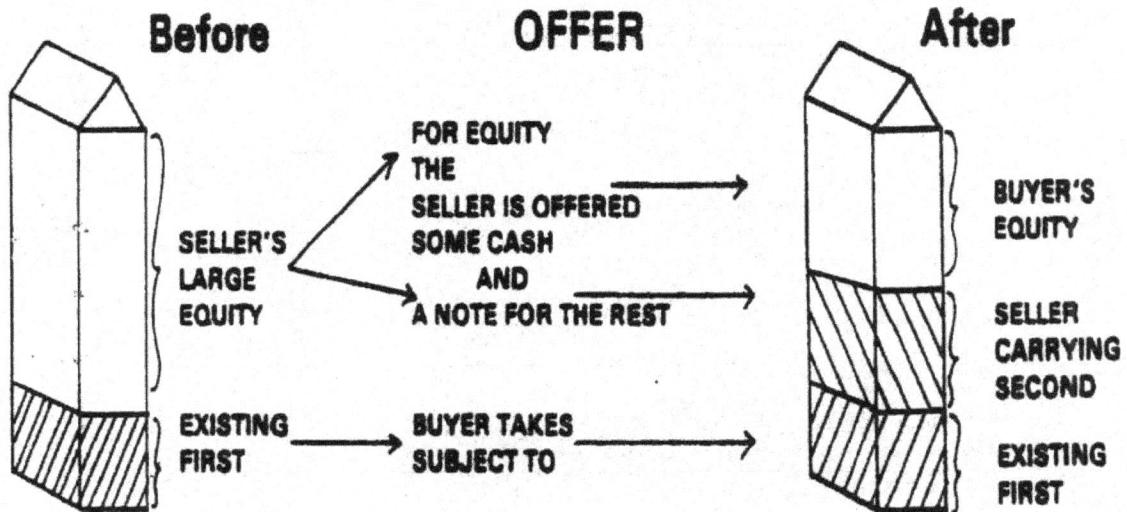

Before   **OFFER**   **After**

SELLER'S LARGE EQUITY

FOR EQUITY THE SELLER IS OFFERED SOME CASH AND A NOTE FOR THE REST

EXISTING FIRST   BUYER TAKES SUBJECT TO

BUYER'S EQUITY

SELLER CARRYING SECOND

EXISTING FIRST

Benefits

To the Purchaser	To the Seller
1. Purchaser can act fast to acquire bargain.	1. Seller received fast action.
2. Seller will be more flexible than other types of lenders on repayment terms.	2. Property is sold.
3. Existing low interest loan can be taken over by buyer.	3. Income from note to supplement other income.
4. Soft loan terms on property make it more resaleable.	4. Note can be traded or used as down payment on another property.

Notes:

_____

_____

_____

_____

_____

_____

_____

Paper out offer

The paper out offer is just as it's name implies. "Give the seller paper (a note and mortgage) and they get out."

It is rare to find a seller that will accept this offer but it does happen. Situations which might arise where this would be an appropriate offer are:

1. The seller does not want a large taxable gain during the current tax year.

2. The seller enjoys monthly income but is tired of management.

3. Seller has run out of time and does not want to take a deep discount for cash.

Offer

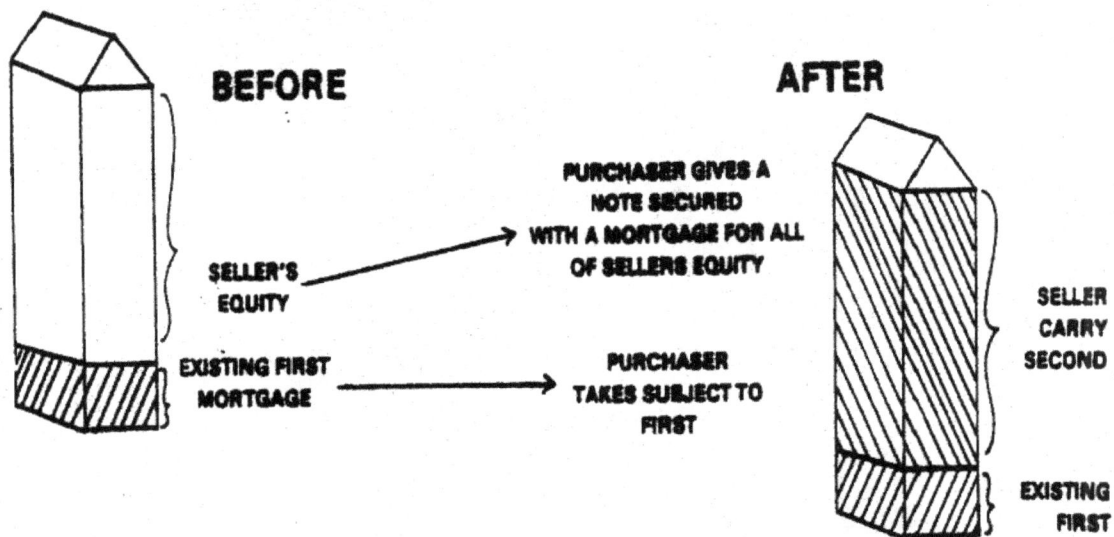

Benefits

To the Purchaser	To the Seller
1. Fast closing. No waiting for bank approval.	1. Seller can still receive income but without management.
2. Purchaser receives better than bank terms.	2. Taxable gain spread out over the life of the note.
3. Minimal closing costs. No loan points.	3. Carry-back note can be sold for cash.

Special Note

There are many variations of the paper out. Some even generate cash for the seller or buyer.

Note again that there are several ways to repay the note to the seller. Choose the one that gives you positive cash flow.

Notes:

_____

_____

_____

_____

_____

Paper out with the carry-back note to be sold for CASH

Many times a seller will offer a discount for cash and fast action. These offered discounts create equity for the buyer which the buyer can use to create the cash for the seller.

This offer is a variation of the paper out offer where it is agreed in the initial offer that the seller carry-back note and mortgage will be sold to an investor at closing. The investor will buy the "carried-back note" at a discounted price, improving the yield on the note, and the seller will receive cash.

Offer

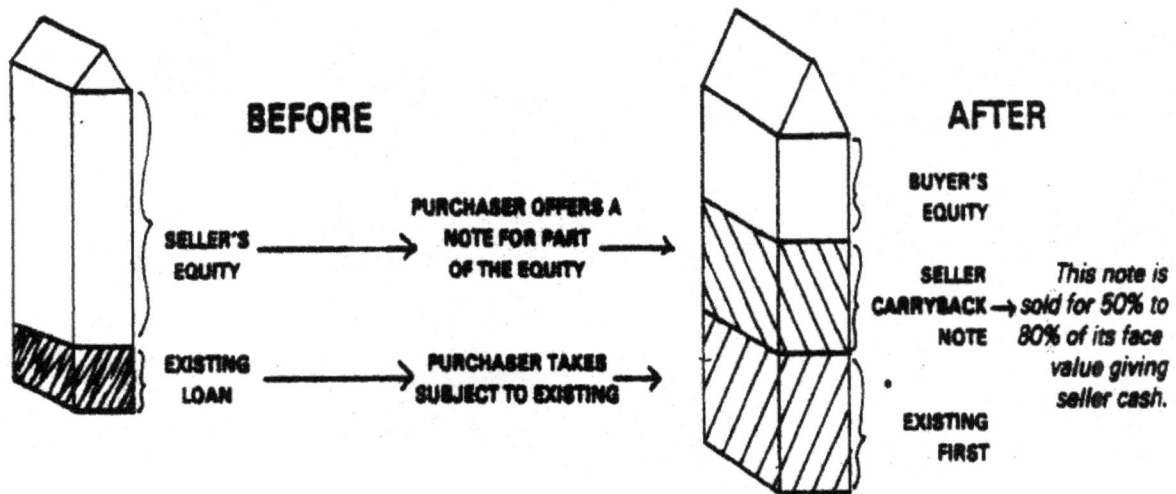

BEFORE

SELLER'S EQUITY → PURCHASER OFFERS A NOTE FOR PART OF THE EQUITY →

EXISTING LOAN → PURCHASER TAKES SUBJECT TO EXISTING →

AFTER

BUYER'S EQUITY

SELLER CARRYBACK → NOTE

EXISTING FIRST

This note is sold for 50% to 80% of its face value giving seller cash.

Benefits

To the Purchaser	To the Seller
1. Purchaser receives all of the Benefits of the paper out.	1. Seller in working with the buyer, receives all cash.
	2. Minimal closing costs.
	3. Fast action.

Special Note

You as the purchaser will want to find the investors who purchase the note to be sure the deal closes. Creative buyers have their partners buy the notes and share in the ownership of their own mortgages.

This type creative offer opens up a whole new field of investing in discounted notes and mortgages (paper). For a complete course on this exciting technique, go to www.megamortgages course.com and www.crackthemortgagecode.com.

Notes:

_____

_____

_____

_____

_____

_____

_____

Paper out with short term balloon note
to be refinanced

Many sellers need cash but not necessarily right away. Some sellers will wait several months for the down payment, and this fact helps you present the following offer. This offer can be used in any situation except when a foreclosure is pending and there is no time to wait for the buyer to raise the cash.

When you purchase a property, the price and down payment are factors in financing at the bank. However, these are not factors when you refinance. Therefore, the buyer takes title first and then refinances to raise cash for the seller and avoids the question of down payment.

Offer

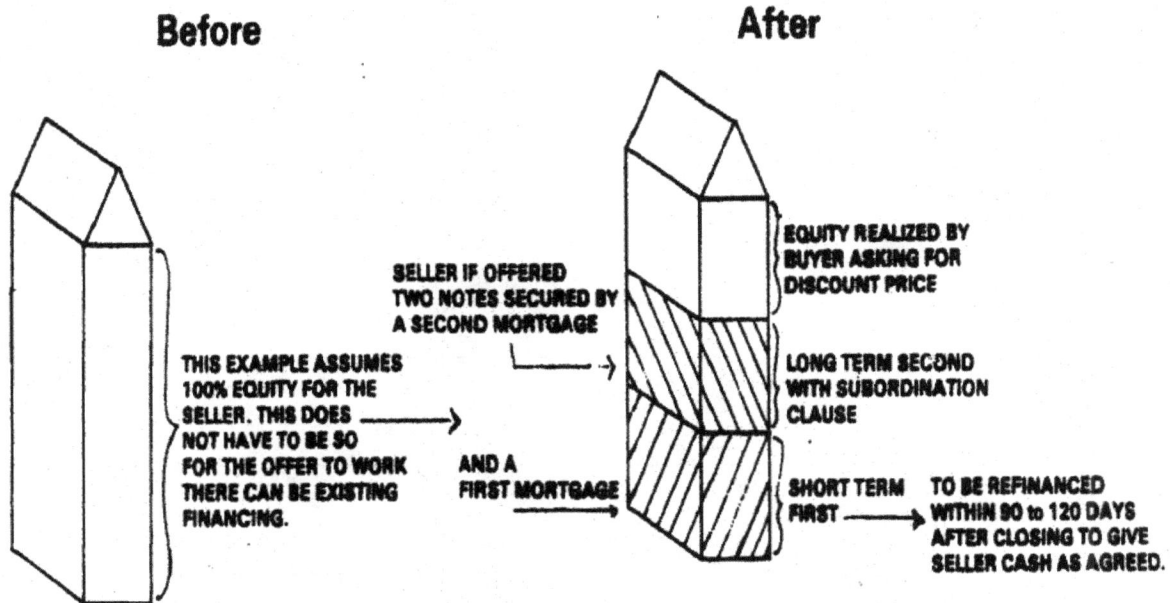

Benefits

To the Purchaser	To the Seller
1. Good Terms.	1. Assured of Sale.
2. No Down Payment.	2. No more wondering.
	3. Seller receives good portion in cash.
	4. Seller can sell, trade or hold paper taken back as a second.

Notes:

_____

_____

_____

_____

_____

_____

_____

Seller refinance
First mortgage crank

Many sellers have large equities in their properties which make them difficult to sell unless they are willing to carry a portion of the equity for the buyer themselves. Creative buyers can use these large equities to generate cash for the seller but are plagued by the problem of the bank wanting to see down payments and wanting buyers to qualify.

Solution: Let the seller refinance with an assumable loan, to raise the cash he needs. Then the buyer simply needs to purchase the property subject to the new loan, and the seller receives a note secured by a second mortgage for the balance of his equity.

This offer can be used in any situation in which the seller has a large equity and good credit. A seller in foreclosure cannot accept this offer as he would be unable to secure the new loan.

Offer

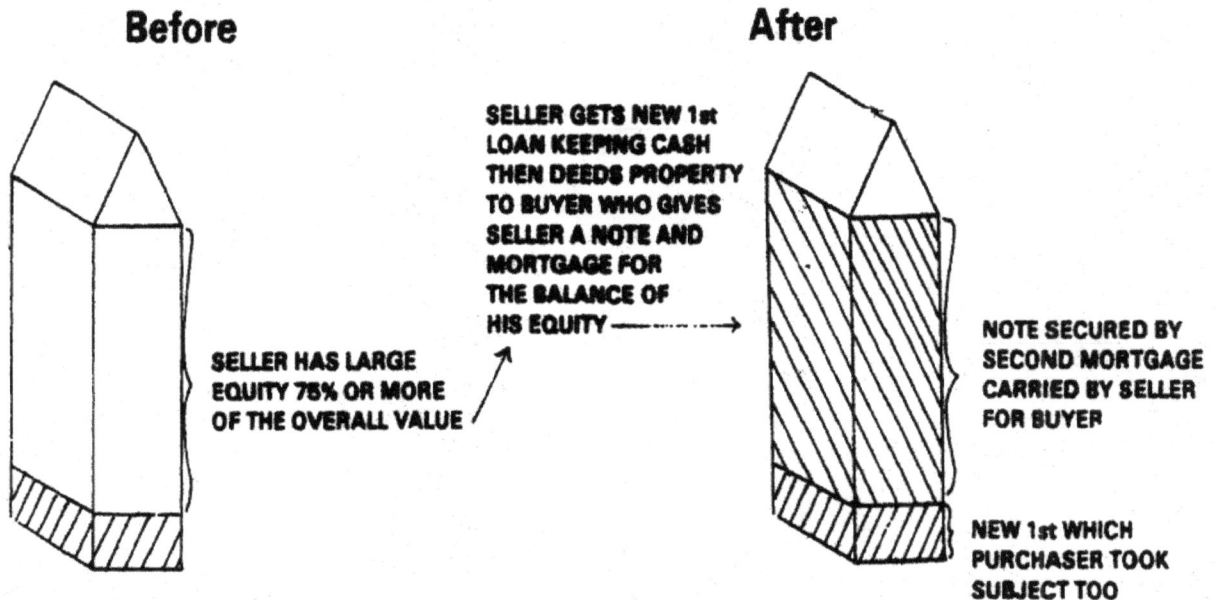

Before

SELLER HAS LARGE EQUITY 75% OR MORE OF THE OVERALL VALUE

After

SELLER GETS NEW 1st LOAN KEEPING CASH THEN DEEDS PROPERTY TO BUYER WHO GIVES SELLER A NOTE AND MORTGAGE FOR THE BALANCE OF HIS EQUITY ------->

NOTE SECURED BY SECOND MORTGAGE CARRIED BY SELLER FOR BUYER

NEW 1st WHICH PURCHASER TOOK SUBJECT TOO

Benefits

1.	Seller solves a frustrating problem – selling with a large equity at a time when buyers are reluctant to refinance.
2.	Second carried back gives seller extra cash flow and defers taxes on resale profits.
3.	Seller can wrap the new first for added security.
4.	The carry-back paper can be traded or sold to meet other needs of the seller.

Special Note

Not every seller will accept an offer like this one. Surprisingly enough, the major reason once explained is that they do not want to be bothered by the inconvenience of going to the bank to apply for a loan. To overcome this objection, have the bank come to the seller. Most lending institutions have persons they call solicitors who will make house calls to take loan applications or this can now be done online with many lending institutions..

Notes:

_____

_____

_____

_____

_____

Seller refinance -
Second mortgage crank

The second mortgage crank can be used to solve the same problems as the first mortgage crank. Use the second mortgage crank approach whenever there is an existing first loan worth keeping in place. For example, if there is a medium or large loan (in relation to overall property value) at a low rate of interest, you would not want to pay it off. Generate cash for the seller by getting a new second or by letting the seller get a new second.

Offer

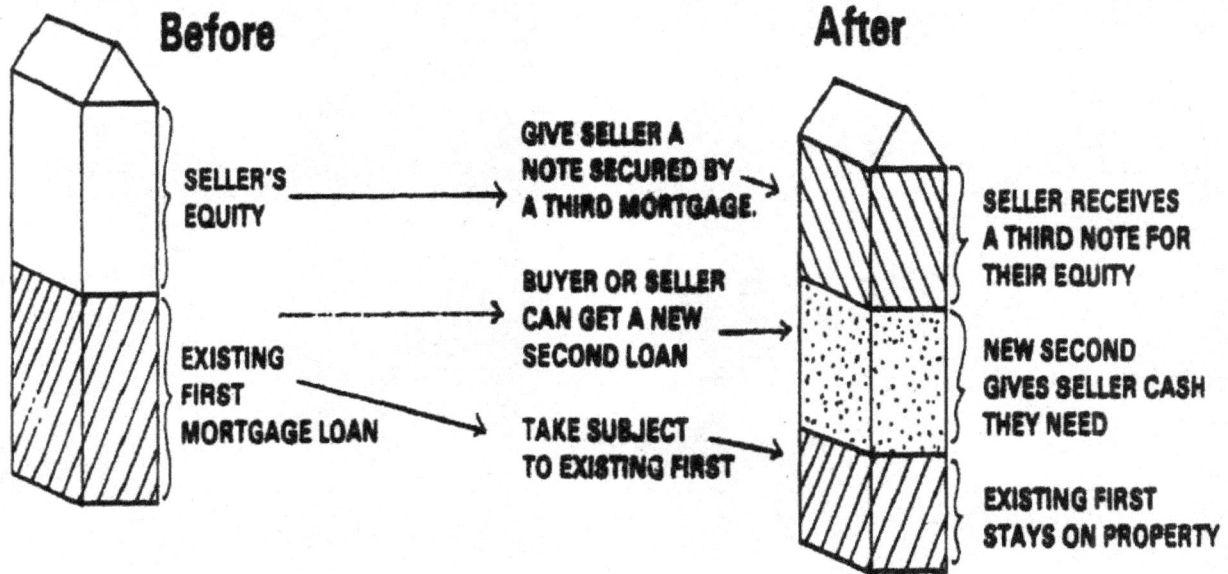

Before

SELLER'S EQUITY

EXISTING FIRST MORTGAGE LOAN

GIVE SELLER A NOTE SECURED BY A THIRD MORTGAGE.

BUYER OR SELLER CAN GET A NEW SECOND LOAN

TAKE SUBJECT TO EXISTING FIRST

After

SELLER RECEIVES A THIRD NOTE FOR THEIR EQUITY

NEW SECOND GIVES SELLER CASH THEY NEED

EXISTING FIRST STAYS ON PROPERTY

Benefits

To the Purchaser	To the Seller
1. Purchaser can take over low interest first mortgage loan.	1. Seller can receive, in some cases, as much as half of their equity in cash.
2. Second mortgage lenders are not as stringent on down payment requirements.	2. Seller defers tax on capital gain.
	3. Seller can sell or carry-back note for more cash.

Notes:

_____

_____

_____

_____

_____

_____

_____

Cash back variation of the first mortgage crank

There are many situations in which, when properly presented, the buyer can receive cash at the closing. This offer is good in several situations. For example when a property is being sold at a below market price, or when there is repair work needed to be performed.

The concept herein is that you are using a mortgage crank offer in which the seller is going to give back cash to the buyer at closing. To get a seller to agree you need a good reason for them to go along such as: some of the money will be used to repair the property, improving their security. Cash can be rebated to hold as reserve for negative cash flow, again improving the seller's security. Give them a reason and they will give you the cash.

Offer

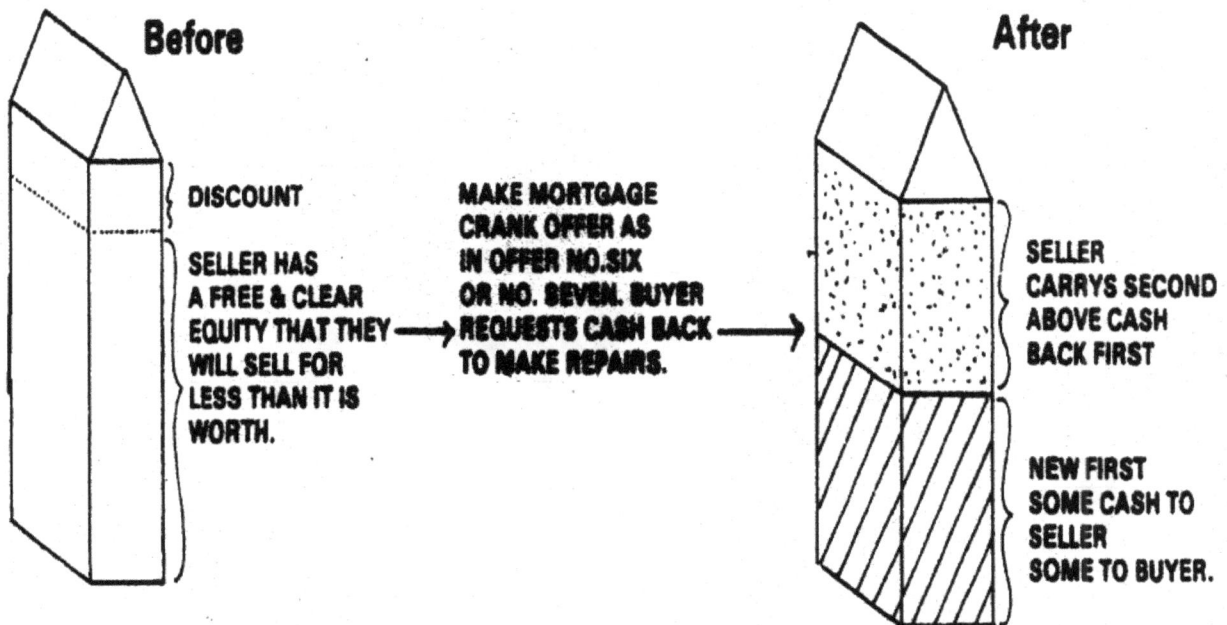

Before

DISCOUNT

SELLER HAS A FREE & CLEAR EQUITY THAT THEY WILL SELL FOR LESS THAN IT IS WORTH.

MAKE MORTGAGE CRANK OFFER AS IN OFFER NO.SIX OR NO. SEVEN. BUYER REQUESTS CASH BACK TO MAKE REPAIRS.

After

SELLER CARRYS SECOND ABOVE CASH BACK FIRST

NEW FIRST SOME CASH TO SELLER SOME TO BUYER.

Benefits

To the Purchaser	To the Seller
1. Buyer receives cash that can be used as a reserve for negative cash flow or for other purposes.	1. Security for the seller's loan is increased when the property is repaired.
	2. Seller receives a good portion of their equity in cash and a sale is made.

Notes:

_____

_____

_____

_____

_____

_____

_____

_____

Created paper down payment

Every time you open a newspaper you can find sellers who are willing to finance a portion of the sale for the buyer. When this occurs, the seller receives a note and some cash. This offer gives the seller exactly that, cash and a note. However, in the case of this offer the note is secured against a property that you already own instead of the property you are buying.

Almost every seller is a candidate for this type of offer. It is especially attractive as a considerable amount of cash can be offered to the seller. The cash is generated by refinancing the property which you are purchasing.

Step one is to create a note against the equity in the property you already own. You need to consult an attorney to insure that this is done properly.

Step two is to offer this note to your seller as part of your down payment.

Step three is to refinance the existing loan of the seller to generate cash for the balance of the purchase price.

Offer

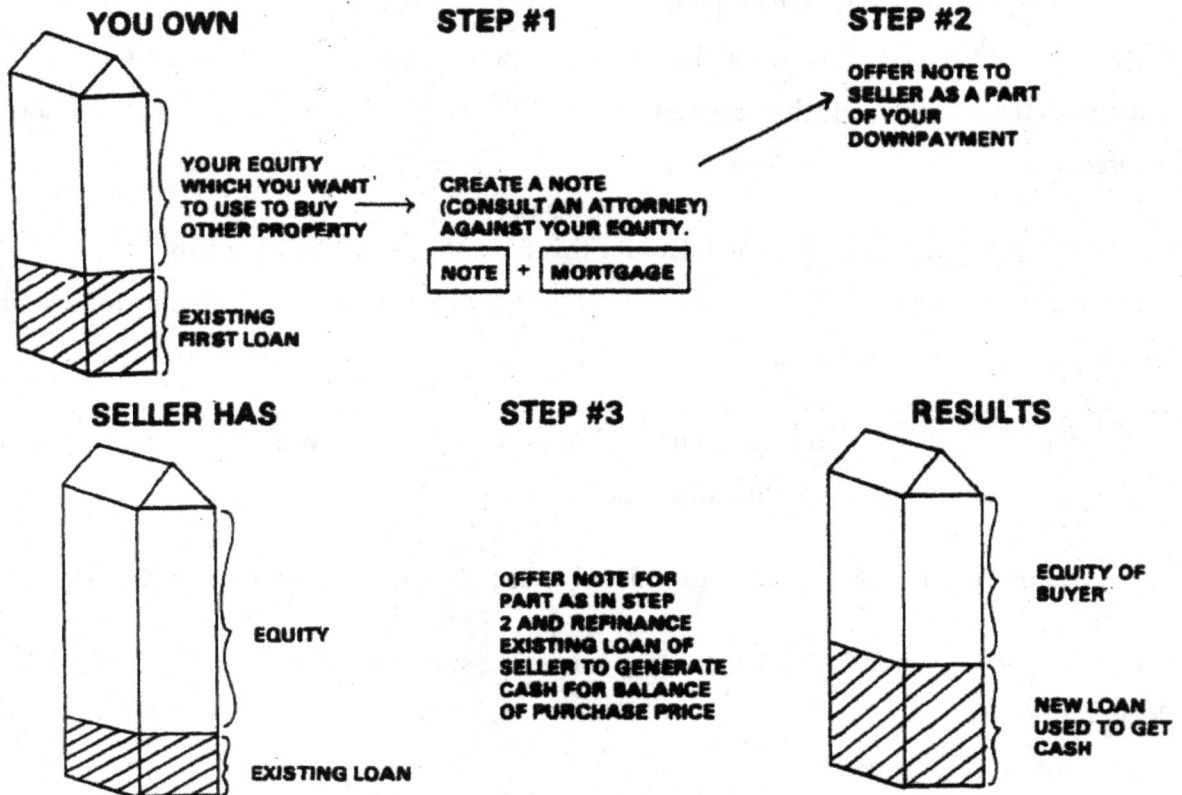

YOU OWN

YOUR EQUITY WHICH YOU WANT TO USE TO BUY OTHER PROPERTY

EXISTING FIRST LOAN

STEP #1

CREATE A NOTE (CONSULT AN ATTORNEY) AGAINST YOUR EQUITY.

NOTE + MORTGAGE

STEP #2

OFFER NOTE TO SELLER AS A PART OF YOUR DOWNPAYMENT

SELLER HAS

EQUITY

EXISTING LOAN

STEP #3

OFFER NOTE FOR PART AS IN STEP 2 AND REFINANCE EXISTING LOAN OF SELLER TO GENERATE CASH FOR BALANCE OF PURCHASE PRICE

RESULTS

EQUITY OF BUYER

NEW LOAN USED TO GET CASH

Special Note:

The buyer ends up with as much equity in the purchased property as he had in the property on which the note is created against. This is because the equity is not spent but simply transferred from the property he owns to the property he is purchasing.

When using this technique be aware of cash flows. You will not only have to support the property you are buying but also the note you have created against your property. This is a minor problem that can be overcome with creative loan structuring.

Paper out offer
subject to seller trading paper

The secret of successful negotiation lies in being able to help the seller accomplish his goals. Many sellers require cash because they feel they need cash to buy their next property. Creative buyers know that this is not the case. Cash isn't the only way to buy.

The concept herein is that if a seller accepts your paper out offer he will receive paper instead of cash. Our offer is made subject to the seller being able to use the carry-back note we are asking him to accept to buy what he needs in the way of replacement property.

The seller accepts your offer, then finds a new property with your help in which he can trade the note as part of his purchase price. If he cannot find a suitable property that will work on a trade, the deal would be called off. If he does find a workable situation, everyone wins.

Offer

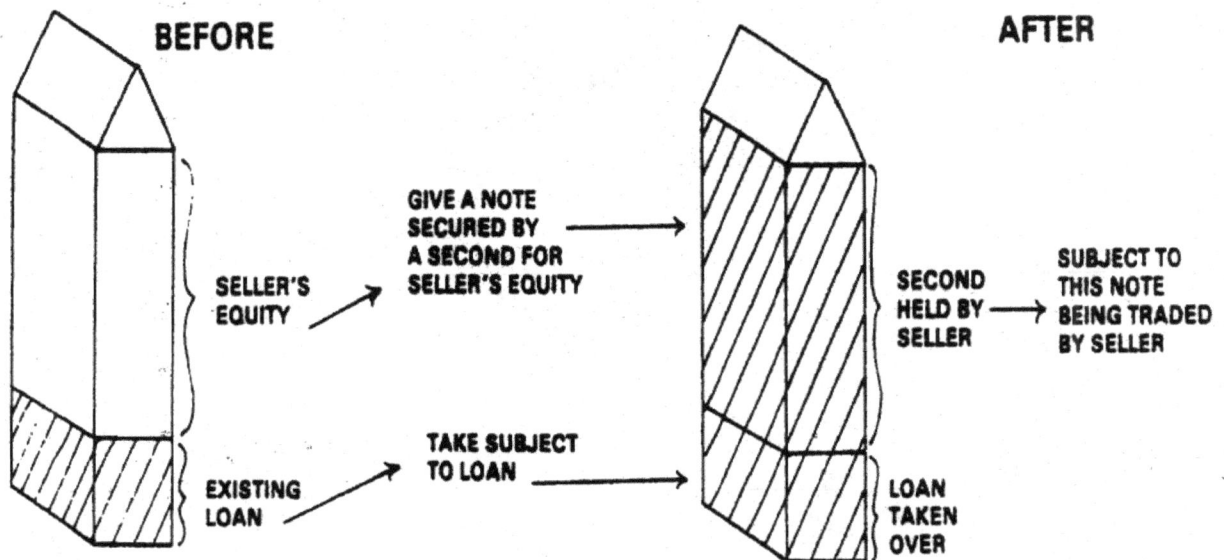

BEFORE

SELLER'S EQUITY → GIVE A NOTE SECURED BY A SECOND FOR SELLER'S EQUITY →

EXISTING LOAN → TAKE SUBJECT TO LOAN →

AFTER

SECOND HELD BY SELLER → SUBJECT TO THIS NOTE BEING TRADED BY SELLER

LOAN TAKEN OVER

Benefits

To the Purchaser	To the Seller
1. Buyer gets in without cash	1. Sale is to seller as if he received all cash. This is so as nothing happens unless the seller can trade the note.
Broker involved is cooperative as there is potential for two sales instead of just one.	

Special Note

This offer is a lesson in negotiation. If you can focus on the needs of the other party and deliver to him what he is looking for, he will give you the deal.

You will need to thoroughly explain this offer to the seller's agent. Be sure that he understands the benefits to his client in this offer. Once he sees the benefits he will get, your offer will be accepted by the seller.

Notes:

_____

_____

_____

_____

_____

Blanket mortgage
combined with a second mortgage crank

The blanket mortgage concept is designed to make a seller feel secure. In effect you are giving the seller a lien against the property you are buying as well as on one you already own.

If the seller's concern in selling to you is that you have nothing invested, and no risk, this offer is obviously ideal.

Offer

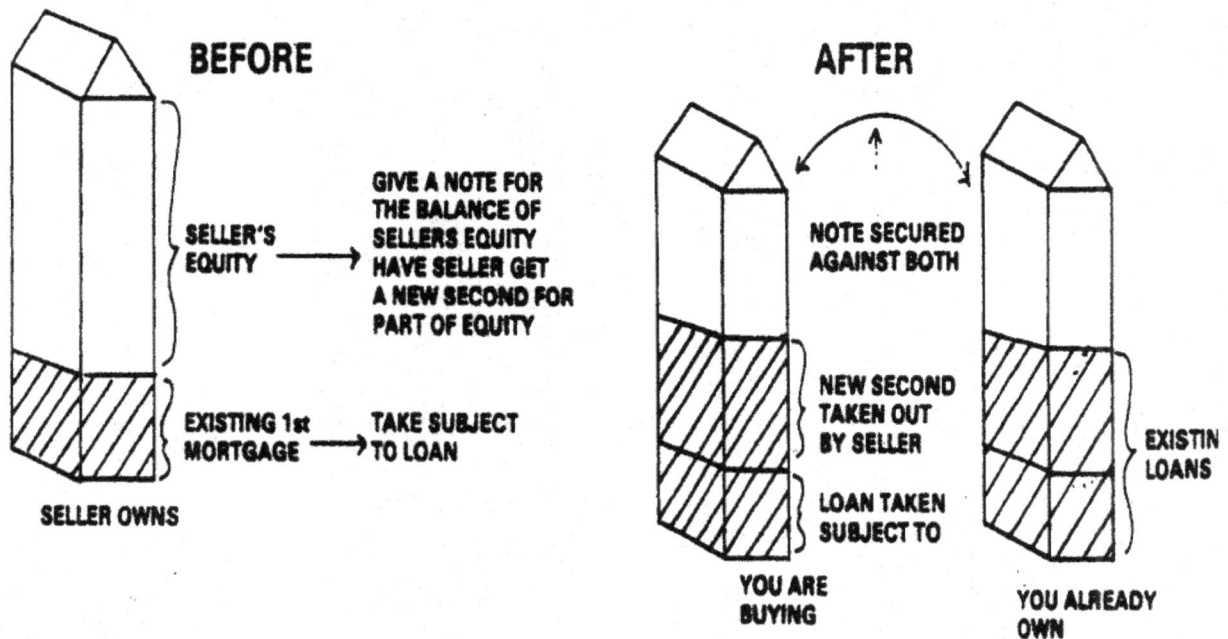

Benefits

1. Additional security for the seller. If the buyer defaults, seller gets two properties.

2. All of the Benefits associated with a blanket mortgage offer.

Special Note

The blanket mortgage is offered to make the seller feel secure. This does not mean that the second property has to remain as collateral for the life of the loan. It can be released prior to note maturity. Negotiate early release clauses which you will find in the glossary.

Notes:

_____

_____

_____

_____

_____

_____

_____

Lease with an option to purchase

The lease with an option to purchase is a powerful tool that buyers can use to control real estate. There are a lot of sellers who will readily accept this type of offer. Many of these sellers advertise in the "Real Estate For Rent" classifieds. The ad will not only offer the property for rent but will also offer an option to purchase. The only items you have to negotiate are the length of the option and the monthly rent.

This offer also makes a great back-up offer. Make one or two offers to purchase. If they are not accepted, then offer the lease option.

Offer

Before   **After**

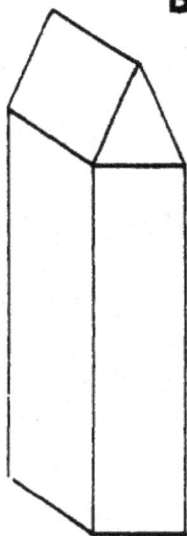

PROPERTY VALUE
$80,000
FAIR MARKET RENT
$600

ASK FOR AN OPTION
TO PURCHASE WITHIN
10 YEARS AT $80,000.
MEANWHILE RENT UNTIL
CLOSING FOR $500 PER
MONTH.

BUYER CONTROLS
PROPERTY AND
APPRECIATION.
BUYER RENTS TO
SUB TENENT FOR
$600 AND EARNS
CASH FLOW.

Benefits

To the Purchaser	To the Seller
1. Purchaser can control property with very little cash.	1. Seller can take depreciation write-offs as the property has changed from residence to investment.
2. Low rent makes it easy to make a profit.	2. A lease with an option offers the same benefit to a seller as a short-term balloon loan. When the option comes due, the seller gets cashed out. This can happen as early as three to five years after the deal is made. The seller's alternative is to demand a balloon loan (same early payout) which buyers do not like, or accept thirty year financing having to wait for their money.
3. The purchaser will have no personal liability as he would with a loan.	3. If the buyer defaults and does not exercise the option, the seller will get the property back

Notes:

_____

_____

_____

_____

_____

_____

Reverse interest loan offer

The reverse interest loan is a method of repaying a debt more than it is an offer to purchase. The purpose of including it in this book was to show how it should be written into an offer for easy explanation.

The reverse interest loan pays off rapidly (in half the time of a conventional loan) and it starts with low payments to give positive cash flow. It can be used virtually any time that you have a seller that will finance.

Negotiating

As you can see in the contract, the loan repayment schedule is laid out in a chart form to facilitate explanation to the seller.

Point to the chart and show the seller the amount of principal they will receive each year and the monthly payments that are used to repay that principal together with interest. It should also be pointed out to the seller that the payments increase each year as additional interest must be paid on the principal for each year the loan is outstanding. The simplest explanation of interest is to explain; "I will pay you more interest each year, the same as the bank pays you more on a passbook account. The longer they hold your money, the more they pay, the same as I am doing with the money I owe you.."

Computing a reverse interest loan

1. Divide the principal amount of the loan by the number of years you wish to repay the loan. The results will equal the annual amount of principal to be repaid.

2. Refer to a payment table book (or use a financial calculator) and determine the monthly payments at the interest rate agreed upon between the buyer and the seller of the annual principal amount amortized over one year.

3. Multiply the annual principal amount of the interest rate stated as a decimal (10% = .10). Then divide by twelve (12). This amount becomes the factor by which each year's payments will increase. (See Example.)

Example

1. $30,000 principal ÷ 15 years = $2,000 annual principal.

2. $2,000 amortized over 1 year at 12% = $177.70 monthly payments.

3. 12% of $2,000 = $240 ÷ $20.00 = annual payment increase.

   i.e.:   Year #1 $177.70
           Year #2 $197.70
           Year #3 $217.70
           Year #4 $237.70

   And continuing until paid in 15 years.

Notes:

_____

_____

_____

_____

_____

Purchased paper as a substitute collateral

How would you like to purchase a property at 30 to 40% below market without asking the seller to discount his price. In addition you could receive cash at the closing and no one would object.

Sounds impossible but it is really rather easy. To do this you will need two things. One, you will need a seller who will finance the sale for you with a reasonable down payment (say 15 to 25%). Two, you will need an understanding of the concepts of buying paper at a discount.

Purchase a note (secured by a mortgage) at a discount and use it as security for carry-back financing which you negotiate with the seller of the real estate. The paper is secured by other real estate offered in lieu of the seller's real estate as collateral for the note.

Offer

To clearly explain this concept values have been included to make the offer clear and easily understood.

STEP #1:   Purchase a secured note from a note holder (typically a private party)

Note Holder Has		You offer
Balance owed on note, $80,000		$40,000 cash in 90 days subject to being able to arrange suitable financing
Interest	10%	
Term	30 years	
Payments	$822.89	

STEP #2 Purchase real estate

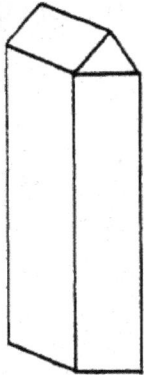

Seller owns
100,000
value

assume
it is free & clear

OFFER
$20,000 cash and an
$80,000 note secured by a
collateral assignment
of the paper you are purchasing

STEP #3   Refinance

To complete the transaction you will need to arrange for financing to be secured against the property you are acquiring.

New Loan	$80,000
Less Cash to Seller	$20,000
Purchase of paper	$40,000
Estimated costs	$ 6,000
Balance	$14,000 Cash in buyer's pocket

Benefits

1. Seller receives at or near his asking price.

2. Seller receives the cash down payment he was asking for.

3. Seller receives a note as he was advertising he would accept.

4. Seller has two people plus real estate securing the note which you are giving; (1) you are signing the note,

   (2) the person who signed the note you are offering as collateral, and

(3) the property securing the note you are offering as collateral, assuming that both you and the signer on the purchased note were to default.

5. There might be a greater amount of equity in the property securing the purchased note making it better collateral than the property the seller is selling.

6. If the note you are buying has been in existence for any length of time it will have a performance record, whereas a new note against his own property will not have any payment record to rely upon.

Notes:

_____

_____

_____

_____

_____

_____

_____

Notes:

Time Value of Money

Money has value over time. The two concepts- money and time- are interrelated and one cannot function without the other. The purchasing power of a dollar today is worth more than the purchasing power of the dollar received in the future. Money loses buying power over time because of inflation. This is because you can invest a dollar today and earn a return or what is called a yield. Which means money is worth more ten years ago because of inflation. Past dollars invested have more buying power than dollars invested today. For example, if you invested a dollar ($1.00) today and earned ten (10%) percent interest, you would have $1.10 at the end of the year.

A lender charges for loss of buying power over time by charging what is called interest. Interest is calculated as a percentage of the remaining unpaid principal balance of the loan over a defined period of time. The dollar amount of interest is a function of three variables: (1) the interest rate (2) the amount borrowed (principal) and (3) the time period of the loan.

There are two types of interest that can be charged: "simple" and "compound."

Simple interest is calculated as follows: principal x interest rate x time. For example, if you borrowed $1,000 for 12 months at 10% simple interest, your interest would be:

Interest= $1,000 x 10% x 12 months = $100 for the 12 months.

Compound interest is the interest that accrues on both the principal and the past-unpaid accrued interest. When interest is compounded, interest is earned for each period on the principal and on the accumulated interest for the preceding periods.

For example, if you borrowed $1,000 for 12 months at 10% compound interest, your total payments would be $87.92 per month x 12 months = $1,054.99.

Financial calculators use a mathematical formula to discount today's dollars to the equivalent future dollars. This time value of money calculation determines the loss of future buying power of money paid in the future.

To determine this number, we use five financial keys on the calculator:

N   **I/Y**   **PV**   **PMT**   **FV**

They represent the following elements of a time-value of money calculation.

N   = the number of payments remaining

I/Y   = effective interest rate per compounding period

PV   = present value of today's dollars

PMT   = the periodic payment amount

FV   = future value of the dollars

What are the key time-value of money characteristics? There are four basic characteristics that create a higher value today: (1) higher interest rate, (2) higher present value amount, (3) shorter length of time to maturity, and (4) more frequent compounding periods.

There are four basic characteristics that create a lower value today: (1) lower interest rate, (2) lower present value amount, (3) shorter length of time to maturity, and (4) less frequent compounding periods.

Our parents always taught us to save our money for the future, or "the rainy day" as they called it. Nobody listened. But, what is the value, or should I say, the cost of not following parental advice?

Let's take an example. Suppose you started investing $100 per month at age eighteen at an 8% return every month until you reached age 30, and then you stopped investing. You simply left the money alone, accumulating interest at 8% until you retired at age 65. What would be the difference if you started investing $100 per month at age 30, and continued to invest $100 per month, every month, at 8% until you retired at age 65? If you started at age 18 and quit at age 30, the total sum would be $1,020,136.80. If you started at age 30 and quit at age 65, the sum would be $229,388.25, a whopping difference of $790,748.55.

Start at Age 18 and Stop at Age 30				
N	**I/Y**	**PV**	**PMT**	**FV**
144	8	0	100	24,050.84
(12 Years)				
N	**I/Y**	**PV**	**PMT**	**FV**
564	0	-24,050.84	0	1,020,136.80
(47 years from age 18 to 65)				
Start at Age 30 and Stop at Age 65				
N	**I/Y**	**PV**	**PMT**	**FV**
420	8	0	100	229,388.25
(35 years)				

Let's look at three reasons why you should buy paper. First of all, you should buy paper for cash flow. If you can go out into the marketplace and find a $5,000 note that calls for payments of $150 a month and you can either buy that note at a discount or lend your $5,000 and receive $150 - that's cash flow to your benefit. The receipt of that money on a monthly basis is your benefit.

There are different types of notes: notes that call for payments are known as installment notes and notes that have no payments, except for a big payment due sometime in the future, are called straight notes. Then there is the combination of the two. A combination could be an interest only loan where you receive the interest payment as an installment, then a straight note balloon payment.

If you are looking for cash flow, obviously, either buy or lend on an installment basis. Don't put all of your eggs into one basket when you are buying notes for cash flow. Either loan money out in small increments for short durations of time or buy notes that are small in nature and have a short duration themselves. If you are buying a loan that already exists, look for one with a balance of $5,000 to $10,000 for a good cash flow. If you are lending, (which for cash flow is probably the best way because you get to pick your own security), you should lend for only a year of two at a time. You might consider lending on the interest only with a balloon payment basis, lending it for a year or two. Lend or buy short remaining terms using smaller sums of money.

If I had $25,000 to invest in the cash flow market, I would prefer to lend it out in five different locations. This way I would be protected if one or two of them should go bad.

Cash flow

If you are investing for a yield, then you should be buying existing notes at a discount. As you would for cash flow, if you are lending in small increments, you should be buying in small increments. Again, I would prefer to buy $5,000 notes rather than one $25,000 note.

If you are buying notes to trade into real estate, you are going to buy the big notes, $15,000 and larger. We'll discuss these techniques as we cover all of the various techniques on how to lend for yield, how to lend for cash flow, how to buy for yield and how to trade for acquiring real estate.

Notes:

_____

_____

_____

_____

_____

_____

_____

Notes:

Inflation

For a dollar value of goods, let's say worth $1,000 worth of goods, if prices are going up, for instance at a rate of 10%, something that costs you $1,000 at the beginning of the year would cost you $1,100 at the end of the year. If you only had $1,000 to start with, you could buy that product. But at the end of the year, you'd be a $100 short because of the effect of inflation. If we have $100 today and we are experiencing a 7% inflation rate, that $100 is worth only $93.46 in goods at the end of the year. You can buy $100 worth of potatoes today, but only $93.46 worth of potatoes in the future. Money obviously has a value by its age.

So the longer you wait for money, to either receive it or to spend it, the greater affect upon the value of that money time will have. If something is worth $100 today, in ten years during which we've been feeling the ravages of 7% inflation for year after year, the $100 is only going to have a value of $50.83.

Notes:

_____

_____

_____

_____

_____

_____

Notes:

_____

_____

_____

_____

_____

_____

_____

_____

_____

_____

Alternative uses

There is another factor that affects your money, one that affects the time value, I call it the alternative use of money. What could you do with that money today? Could you make it grow? I could put $1,000 into the stock market and make it grow over a year if everything is in my favor. Or, I could put it into a life insurance policy, or even a savings account. The return depends on the interest rate. But I am going to get paid interest. So, if I am experiencing 7% inflation on my $100 and have only $93.00 worth of purchasing power in a year, earning 5.25% does not get me out of the red. I still have an actual loss from not having had the use of the money at the beginning. If I had to wait for it, I've lost the return I could have received. The longer you have to wait to receive an income, the less valuable that income is to you.

If you have the money today, you can double the value of the money by being able to take advantage of the discount. Time has a direct effect on money and it's important that you understand the concept because as we get into discounting and I give you actual examples, you'll be able to follow the time element in your mind and then you'll be able to follow the reasoning of the examples.

Notes:

_____

_____

_____

_____

_____

Notes:

What is discounted paper?

When I use the term "Paper" I am referring to buying notes secured by real estate. These notes or I.O.U.'s usually take the form of a Trust Deed Note, Mortgage Note or Contract for Deed. Besides real estate paper, there are many different types and forms of paper.

Paper is usually bought or sold at a discount. The more you discount the face value of the paper, the higher the rate of return or "yield." For example, if a note of $10,000.00 with an interest rate of 10% were to be bought for a lesser amount, the yield would be higher than the interest rate of 10%.

Many people are not thrilled with math. Of necessity, a book about "paper" deals with many facts and figures, but there is one sure way to make the math exciting: by understanding and using the math, you can make outstanding profits. And when you get excited about these concepts, you will learn to love math.

Instead of watching your favorite TV show, you will find yourself sitting in the corner with a silly grin on your face punching away furiously at the buttons on your calculator. When you get hopelessly addicted, you'll sit back smiling as your calculator shows you how much money you can make. Then, when transactions actually happen, you'll create another ear-to-ear grin as the numbers you see are real. So, forget you ever disliked math, because your calculator is about to become your best friend.

Notes:

_____

_____

_____

_____

_____

_____

_____

_____

_____

_____

$1,000,000 for retirement?

Investing as little as $200 per month can build to a return of over a million dollars by retirement. All that is needed is a safe investment that takes advantage of the principals of "compounding and discounting." There is little knowledge in the financial world more valuable than the knowledge of the time value of money.

Baron Von Rothschild described compound interest as the "eighth wonder of the world." You can use the time value of money to your advantage. No other principle can aid you more powerfully in your financial goals.

Notes:

_____

_____

_____

_____

_____

_____

_____

Notes:

Hey buddy can you spare a trillion?

A good example of compound interest would be to look at the amount of money paid for Manhattan. The Indians sold the land for approximately $24 in trinkets. If that money had been invested at only 7% interest, it would have grown to 1.67 trillion dollars today.

Now, let's say that instead of selling it, they decided to borrow the money and pay 7% interest, with a balloon payment due in 1995. The holder of the note wants to sell it at a 9.28% yield. What would you offer for the note that will balloon at over 1,670,000,000,000 dollars? (At the time of origination).

Would 1 penny seem like a bargain. Only if 9.28% interest is acceptable to you.

$151 for $10,000?

What would you pay me today if I gave you $10,000 in one year? How about 5, 10, 15, 20, 25 or 30 years? If you want a 15% rate or return, you would pay the following amounts (rounded to the nearest dollar).

$ 8,696 for 1 year   a 13% discount

$ 4,972 for 5 years   a 50% discount

$ 2,472 for 10 years   a 75% discount

$ 1,229 for 15 years   an 88% discount

$ 611 for 20 years   a 94% discount

$ 304 for 25 years   a 97% discount

$ 151 for 30 years   a 98% discount

As you can see, the value of a lump sum of cash or a cash flow diminishes rapidly with time. Few people have any grasp of how much. Your powerful tool will be in understanding and being able to calculate exactly how much. Let's look at one more example.

A Penny a Day

Let's say you are offered either $10,000 cash or a salary of 1 penny per day that doubles each day for 30 days (meaning you would receive $.02 the next day, $.04 the third day, etc.) Which would you take? What if you were offered $100,000 cash? One million? Ten million?

Even $ 10,000,000 cash wouldn't equal the total salary amount of $10,737,418.23 that you would receive over the 30 day period.

Notes:

_____

_____

_____

_____

_____

_____

_____

_____

How to discount paper

A payment on a note breaks down into principal and interest. For example, a payment of $130.00 per month may break down into $46.67 principal and $83.33 interest. When the same note is bought at a discount, the payment breaks down into principal, interest and discount. When you calculate your return, you will figure your discount (yield) in the same place you previously calculated the interest.

Discounting involves finding the **"present value"** of a single or series of payments. To do this, the first step is to identify the various series of payments or **"cash flows."** There are three types of cash flows and a note may have only one type or it may have several of each type of cash flow. These three types are:

SINGLE payment

SERIES of payments

SERIES of payments that begins at a FUTURE date.

The series of payments must be the same amount each time and must have an equal period of time in between each one.

There are two basic ways to determine the price and yield of discounted paper. The first and best way to discount cash flows is to use a financial calculator.

The second way to discount cash flows involves yield tables of one kind or another. I highly recommend using a financial calculator. The examples in this book will be much easier to follow with a calculator. Very few individuals still use yield. tables. The steps in using the different calculators may vary, but the process is the same.

If you are interested in becoming highly proficient in this arena of investing, it is recommended that you take the Mega Mortgages course. This is a four day live seminar which covers every aspect of investing in discounted notes and mortgages.

In the examples that we use, the interest rate will usually be an annual interest rate divided by 12. This will make the figures more readable. It is important, however, to know that a change may need to be made. If a note has a monthly payment, all figures should be entered in as monthly figures. For example, if a note has terms like the one shown below, the interest rate should not be entered as 10%, but should be divided by 12 to be able to enter in a monthly figure (.83). If a note has semi-annual. payments, then the terms must reflect that fact. In this case, the interest rate would be 5% and the "N" would be 60 (30 years with 2 payments per year).

Notes:

_____

_____

_____

_____

_____

_____

_____

_____

Interest vs. Price

In calculating the yield on paper, it is easier to think of how the interest rate affects the price or value of a note. The higher the interest rate (yield), the lower 'the value of a payment over a period of time. Let's take as an example a payment of $400.00 per month for 360 months. Below is a chart that shows how much that payment is worth at different interest rates.

%I	PMT	PV	FV	N
8/12	400.00	-54,513.40	N/A	360
10/12	400.00	-45,580.33	N/A	360
12/12	400.00	-38,887.33	N/A	360
14/12	400.00	-33,758.93	N/A	360
16/12	400.00	-29,745.15	N/A	360
18/12	400.00	-19,983.97	N/A	360

Once you grasp the concept of discounting, the whole world of discounted paper and interest rates and yields will become very simple to you. The whole purpose of discounting is to make it so that a note with a lower interest rate than the yield required can still produce that yield. If the person buying the $54,513.40 note in the first line wanted it at a 24% yield, he would have to buy it at the $19,983.97 figure in the bottom line.

Notes:

_____

_____

_____

Notes:

_____

_____

_____

_____

_____

_____

_____

_____

_____

_____

Amortization examined

As mentioned, a payment on a note breaks down into principal and interest. The lower the interest rate, the more of the payment will go to reduce the principal balance. At first, the amount going to reduce the principal balance may seem ridiculous. Since the principal is reduced some, on the next payment the amount used to pay interest is a little bit less and the amount going to principal is a little more. As the payments progress, the principal (or loan balance) begins to reduce much more rapidly until the last payment, when a very small amount goes to pay interest and the balance pays off the principal entirely.

Notes:

Notes:

_____

_____

_____

_____

_____

_____

_____

_____

_____

Discounting - as easy as 1 , 2 , 3

Learning discounting by using a financial calculator can be one of the most important things an investor can do. In the field of real estate and real estate paper, knowledge of discounting is very valuable and can be quite easy.

Discounting and understanding present and future value takes as much as a full week in some courses, so to tackle it is a challenge.

At the same time, I have learned through the courses, seminars and workshops that I teach, that discounting can be presented in an easily understandable way. Any note can be discounted in three easy steps - USING A FINANCIAL CALCULATOR. Do not attempt to do these functions with anything but a financial calculator. People try and then they ask me for the formulas, assuming they' need them or could even understand them.

All you need to know is what number needs to be entered into what key. Just push the number then push the key. That's all there is to it.

Some rules for discounting

1. THE CALCULATOR DOES ALL OF THE WORK

There is no special formula or technical math background that you need. The formulas are built into "financial" calculators.

2. CONSISTENT TIME PERIOD, RATE AND PAYMENT

If the payment is on a monthly basis, then the interest rate must be entered as a monthly interest rate

Example: 12% annual rate breaks down to 1% per month) and the number of payments must be a total monthly figure

Example: 10 years would be 120 months). If the payment is on a semi-annual basis, then the interest rate and time period should reflect that.

Example: 12% per year = 6% per semi-annual period. 10 years worth of payments at twice a year would be 20).

3. BE CAREFUL TO ENTER ZEROS

Many of the mistakes you might make will come from the fact that most calculators will hold .the numbers in the memory register until they are replaced or cleared. There are five keys on the calculator: N, %I, PMT, PV, FV. Only four keys will be used at one time and the fifth key may need to have a zero entered or the calculations will be off. In order for your calculations to be correct, enter the zero first.

4. LONG AND SHORT EQUALS LARGE AND SMALL

Long term loans require large discounts, because the discount has to apply over a longer period of time to equal a certain yield. Short 'term loans require a smaller amount of discount.

5. DISCOUNT AND YIELD ARE NOT SYNONYMOUS

Many people confuse these two terms. Discount is the amount that must be subtracted from a loan balance to equal the purchase price that should be paid to obtain a certain yield. Yield is the effective rate of return that is produced when less than the face value of a note •is paid in a cash purchase.

6. ROUNDING

Different calculators can round numbers such that you may come up a few cents or a few dollars less or more. If your answer is this close, don't worry.

7. BEGIN/END KEY

If your calculator has this setting, make sure ,it is set on "end" for all of our calculations.

Notes:

Notes:

Three easy steps

Discounting can be as easy as three, simple steps. These steps will work on any brand of financial calculator. Some calculators may do them a lot quicker. When you learn to use the calculator more efficiently, by all means, use those quicker methods.

1. IDENTIFY ALL OF THE CASH FLOWS

2. SOLVE FOR UNKNOWN FACTORS

3. DISCOUNT AND ADD THE CASH FLOWS

There are three types of cash flows that you will deal with. Each note that you want to discount may have one or more of any one or all three cash flows. Here are the different cash flows:

1. SERIES OF PAYMENTS

2. LUMP SUM PAYMENT

3. FUTURE SERIES OF PAYMENTS

A SERIES OF PAYMENTS is where the same amount is paid in regular intervals for a period of time. A LUMP SUM PAYMENT is where only one payment is received at a certain time in the future. A FUTURE SERIES is where there is a series of payments that do not begin immediately, but start at a later date.

Step 1: Dissecting Cash Flows

Let's start with Step 1 and look at a few notes as examples. The first question is:

1. "How many cash flows are there?" The next question is:

2. "What are the cash flows?" The third question is:

3. "What type of cash flow?" The cash flow is determined by how much you receive and when you receive it or how many times you receive it.

EXAMPLE 1: This note has a balance of $10,000.00 and pays $132.15 per month for 10 years at 10% interest.

1. How many cash flows? In this note there is one cash flow.

2. The cash flow is $132.15 per month for 10 years (120 months).

3. This cash flow is a **SERIES OF PAYMENTS** - More than one identical payment ($132.15 per month) occurring at regular intervals (once per month for 120 months).

EXAMPLE 2: This note has a balance of $10,000,00 and has no payments for five years. The interest of 10% adds on each year and in five years there is a balloon payment of $16,105.10.

In this note, there is only one cash flow.

The cash flow is one payment of $16,105.10 in five years.

Since there is only one payment at a future date, this is a **LUMP SUM PAYMENT** type cash flow.

EXAMPLE 3: This note has a balance of $10,000.00 and no payments for three years with interest at 10 percent. In three years the balance will have grown to $13,310.00 (based on annual compounding), at which time there will be payments of $143.03 per month for the next 15 years (a total of 18 years).

In this note there is only one cash flow.

The cash flow is $143.03 per month for 180 months that **begins in three years**.

Since there is a series of payments ($143.03 per month for 180 months) that does not begin until a future date, then this is a **FUTURE SERIES OF PAYMENTS** type cash flow.

EXAMPLE 4: This note has a balance of $10,000.00 and interest at 10%. There are payments of $87.76 per month for the first five years (60 months) and then the entire remaining balance of $9,657.21 will be paid.

There are two cash flows to this note.

The first cash flow (CF1) is $87.76 per month for 60 months. The second cash flow (CF2) one payment of $9,657.21 payable in five years.

The cash flows are:

CF1 = SERIES OF PAYMENTS

CF2 = LUMP SUM PAYMENT

Simplifying the creative confusion

As you can see in the examples just mentioned, it can be simple (with a little practice) to separate the cash flows. You may have seen notes out there in the market place (or created them) that could end up being many cash flows. When a note can be dissected in this way it can help to simplify the complex notes. I realize some of your financial calculators may be able to eliminate some of these steps, but not all of them can. Also, the world of "PAPER" has changed to one where parts and portions of notes are bought and sold. If learned in this way, discounting can be very simple and valuable.

We have discussed the first step of discounting, which is to identify the number and types of cash flows. If there are any unknown factors (such as the length of a series of payments or what a balloon payment will be) then we would go to Step 2 which is to find out these unknown factors. If all factors needed for discounting are known, then we could just go on to Step 3.

Step 2: Uncovering Unknown Factors

The next step in discounting is to discover any unknown factors. In identifying the cash flows, you may need to identify one of the factors with an "X" or another variable, because it is not known at that time.

For example, let's say you have a $10,000.00 note payable $100 per month at 10% interest. How many months will it pay?

At this point we do not know. I would identify the cash flow at first as $100 per month for X months. That determination is good enough for the first step. Now that we are into the second step, we need to find out what X is. The following form is one that will make discounting very easy. The columns correspond to the keys on a financial calculator. The keys are as follows:

(N)   Number, indicating the number of payments, years or time periods.

(%I)   Interest rate or rate of return (yield).

(PMT)   Payment

(PV)   The present value (value at a particular rate of return or yield) or balance.

(FV)   The future value, generally indicating a value, payment or balance at a future date.

Notes:

_____

_____

_____

_____

_____

_____

_____

Notes:

_____

_____

_____

_____

_____

_____

_____

_____

_____

_____

How to lower your house payment

By borrowing some of the equity out of a house and investing it at a higher rate than it is borrowed at, it can create a nice cash flow profit.

Here is an example:

BEFORE		AFTER
$100,000.00	Value	$100,000.00
$ 20,000.00	Loan	$ 80,000.00
$ 167.29	Payment	$ 947.90
-0-	Payment Difference	$ 780.61
8.0%	Interest Rate	14.0%
-0-	Income at 24%	$ 1,136.91
-0-	Cash Flow Difference	$ 356.30
-0-	Net Monthly Income	$ 189.01

Before, there was a payment of $167.29 and now after the refinance and purchase of the paper, the out of pocket payment is totally eliminated and there is a net monthly income of $189.01

Notes:

How to pay off your house early with no payment increase

To pay your house off early, you would need to follow the same procedure as in the previous example. Instead of using the profit to lower the amount that you would have to pay monthly and spending the excess, the profit could be used to pay down the principal balance on the loan. In the example above, if this were done, the loan would pay off in 148 months instead of 360 months which it would have taken with the original loan.

Notes:

_____

_____

_____

_____

_____

_____

_____

Notes:

_____

_____

_____

_____

_____

_____

_____

_____

_____

_____

Building your net worth before you even get richer

By buying paper at a discount, the discount in the face value shows up as an asset on your financial statement. In the previous example, if the paper was bought at a 40 percent discount, the net worth would have been increased by $54,700.00. The original equity in the property was $80,000.00. After the new loan, the property only had $20,000.00 in equity, but there was $94,700.00 in equity in the paper.

Notes:

_____

_____

_____

_____

_____

_____

_____

_____

Notes:

Popping balloons for profit and peace of mind

By a gradual yearly increase in the payment on a note, the amortization length can be greatly reduced and can eliminate the need for a balloon payment. This can be a very attractive opportunity whether a person is paying on the note or receiving payments. If a person is paying on a note, the security, and peace of mind of not having to worry about the balloon payment is well worth the gradual payment increase and may make a property more saleable. If a person is receiving payments on a note, eliminating the balloon payment may make the note more valuable and more saleable. For example, a $10,000.00 note bearing interest at 10% with a 30 year amortization would have a payment of $87.76 per month. If this note had a five year balloon, the amount would be $9,657.43.

If the payment graduated just $30.00 each year, the note would be completely paid at the end of six years. This would also raise the present value of the note from $6,344.84 to $6,909.91 based on a 24% yield. If the payment graduated just $40.00 per year, the note would amortize in just over five years and would be worth $7,198.79, (for a complete breakdown see the chart). The increase in the payment in the first year is a 34% increase. This may not look too attractive, but it may look much more attractive than a $9,657.43 balloon. The concept does not have to have equal or even steady increases to work. Unless you program a computer to do the work, you will just have to experiment and play around with the numbers to find out what will work

The following example shows how to determine how long a $30.00 per year increase in a payment will take to amortize the loan. The first step is to figure the amount of the principal balance after the first year of payments. The new balance is brought down to the next line, the interest rate stays the same, the payment is increased and the calculator solves for how long the loan would now take to amortize. The balance after one year's worth of payments is then calculated and brought down to the next line, the payment increased and etc.

$30/year graduation to pop a 5 year balloon

%I	PMT	PV	FV	N
10	87.76	10,000.00	N/A	360.5
10	117.76	10,000.00	N/A	148.2
10	147.79	9,567.45	N/A	93.46
10	177.76	8,712.59	N/A	63.26
10	207.76	7,391.26	N/A	42.37
10	237.76	5,554.60	N/A	26.09
10	267.76	3,148.65	N/A	12.43
10	113.80	113.80	N/A	1

Notes:

_____

_____

_____

_____

_____

_____

_____

Increasing your yield

Another way to increase your profit is to increase your yield. Your yield can be increased by receiving your original investment and your profit back sooner. For example, if your yield on a note is based on a payment of $100.00 per month and the payment were to be increased to $200.00 per month-your yield has increased tremendously.

As always, there needs to be a benefit for the person paying on the note before they will make changes. Many financial institutions are sending out letters to the people paying on notes and showing them how much sooner their loan will pay off by adding some more to their payment each month. This will save the person paying on the note a lot of money in the long run. Let's look at what. $50.00 increases will do.

Increasing the payment ($50 increments)

1st the original note. "FV" column shows total of payments

I	PMT	PV	FV	N
10	107.46	10,000.00	19,342.80	180.00
10	157.46	10,000.00	14,294.22	90.78
10	207.46	10,000.00	12,839.70	62.89
10	257.46	10,000.00	12,134.09	63.26

As you can see, the loan will pay off much sooner and the person paying on the note will save a lot of money. Where the future value column usually is, is shown the total of the payments. The savings are shown below.

INCREASE	SAVES	PAYS OFF LOAN
$ 50.00	$5,048.58	7.4 years earlier
$100.00	$6,503.i0	9.8 years earlier
$150.00	$7,208.71	11.1 years earlier

Let's look at what this would do to the yield and value of the note. In the "FV" column is that value that the note would have at the same yield it was bought at (24%) and in the "I" column is the new yield on the note, based on what we paid for it.

Increased payment/yield/value

I	PMT	PV	FV	N
24	107.46	5,220.88	(Orig Note)	180
33.14	157.46	5,220.88	6,567.58	90.78
42.02	207.46	5,220.88	7,327.63	61.89
50.79	257.46	5,220.88	7,810.63	47.13

Here is how much each change would increase the value of the note. For a quick profit, you could resale the note at the higher value shown above and realize the profit shown below, although a better option would be to sell a partial interest in the note or to get a loan against the note.

INCREASE IN PAYMENT	INCREASE IN VALUE
$ 50.00	$1,347.70
$100.00	$2,106.75
$150.00	$2,589.75

Lower interest--higher payment

If the savings alone are not enough to entice the "payor" to increase the payment, don't worry--we know how to increase our odds. We can give away some of our profit to the "payor" and increase their motivation. If we lower the interest rate, they will save more money and be more likely to make the change. We will still increase our yield dramatically. In the following example we, lower the interest rate 2% for every $50.00 increase in the monthly payment There is nothing magical about these particular figures--it is simply a matter of negotiation between you and the "payor". The first line below shows the original note. The payment total is shown in the "FV" column.

I	PMT	PV	FV	N
10	107.46	10,000.00	19,342.80	180
8	157.46	10,000.00	13,047.14	82.86
6	207.46	10,000.00	11,470.76	55.29
4	257.46	10,000.00	10,728.36	41.67

Your new yield

As mentioned, this would raise your yield on the note quite a bit. In the example below, we will look at the difference in the yield as well, as the differences in the value of the note. Because of the increased yield and value, an investor could even sell the note again for a profit if he wanted to. The new value of the note is .shown in the "FV" column.

I	PMT	PV	FV	N
32.1	157.46	5,220.88	6,347.09	82.86
39.8	207.46	5,220.88	6,902.43	55.29
47.4	257.46	5,220.88	7,232.59	41.67

Turning long term paper to short term

You may want to use these same principals to turn long term paper 'into short term paper even if the increase in the yield is not substantial. By doing this, it will increase your cash flow and make your paper more saleable or loanable. For example, if you doubled the payment on the following note and cut the interest rate to 0%, the term would shorten from ten years to just over three years and the yield would increase to 35%. Here's the example.

First--the Original Note

I	PMT	PV	FV	N
10	132.15	10,000.00	N/A	120
0	264.30	10,000.00	N/A	37.84
24	132.15	5,993.75	(cost of note)	120
35.19	264.30	5,993.75	(yield at 0%)	37.84

Notes:

Glossary of real estate financial terms

Abstract of Title - A summary of all the recorded instruments and proceedings that affect the title to property, arranged in the order in which they were recorded.

Accelerate - To make a debt due and payable at once.

Acceleration Clause - A provision in a note, mortgage or trust deed that permits the holder to declare the entire unpaid balance due and payable at once upon the happening of some particular event, such as failure to pay an installment on time or sale of the property used as security.

Accrued interest - Interest that has been earned but is not due and payable.

Acknowledgment - A formal declaration before an authorized official (usually a notary public) by the person who executed a document stating that he did in fact execute it. The notary public signs and puts his seal on a written statement describing the declaration. This written statement, or acknowledgment, is required on most instruments before they may be recorded.

All-Inclusive Contract of Sale, Mortgage or Trust Deed - See Wrap-Around Contract of Sale, Mortgage or Trust Deed.

ALTA Title Insurance Policy - A type of title insurance issued to lenders that gives greater coverage than a standard policy by insuring against additional items, such as unrecorded physical easements, unrecorded mechanic's liens, water and mineral rights, facts a physical survey would not show, and rights of persons in possession. Formerly called ATA title insurance policy. ALTA is an abbreviation for American Land Title Association, a trade association of title insurance companies.

Amortization - The repayment of a debt in installments.

Amortized Loan - A loan that is completely paid off in installments.

Amortized Note - A promissory note that is completely paid off in installments.

Annual Statement - A statement required by some state statues to be given by a note holder to the payer within 60 days after the end of each year itemizing and accounting for the money received during the year just ended.

Appraisal Report - The report, written by a real estate appraiser, stating the appraiser's opinion of the value of real property.

Appraised Value - An estimate or opinion of value at a stated time. The opinion of value expressed by a real estate professional known as a real estate appraiser.

Assessed Value -The value placed on property for taxation purposes.

Assessor - An official who has the responsibility of determining assessed value.

Assign - To transfer title to personal property or a right or claim to another person.

Assignee - A person to whom title to personal property or a right or claim is transferred.

Assignment - A transfer by one person (the assignor) to another (the assignee) of title to personal property.

Assignor - A person who transfers title to personal property or a right or claim to another person.

Assume - To take over the obligation of another, for example, to assume a note and deed of trust.

Assumption Agreement - An agreement under which a person (usually a buyer) "assumes" (that is, agree to pay) a note and mortgage or deed of trust on a property.

Balloon Payment - A final installment payment, larger than previous installments, that pays off a debt.

Bene Statement - See Beneficiary Statement.

Beneficiary - The person entitled to the benefit of a trust. In a trust deed the beneficiary is the creditor who is secured and for whose benefit the trustee holds legal title.

Beneficiary Statement - A statement by the holder of a deed of trust stating the amount of the unpaid principal on the note and other information about the debt. The holder is required to give this statement upon payment of a small fee. Also called an offset statement or a bene statement.

Blanket Mortgage or Blanket Trust Deed - A mortgage or deed of trust covering more than one piece of property. For example, it may cover an entire subdivision and provide for a partial reconveyance of individual lots as they are sold.

Call - to declare the entire debt due at once.

Certificate of Discharge - A written instrument executed by the mortgagee and given to the mortgagor when the debt secured by a mortgage is satisfied to show that the mortgage is released. Sometimes called a release of mortgage.

Certificate of Sale - A certificate issued to the buyer at an execution sale or judicial foreclosure sale. The holder of the certificate is entitled to a deed if the owner of the property does not redeem it within 1 year in some states.

Closing Statement - A statement from an escrow agent given to the parties at closing when it is closed, accounting for all funds received into and paid out of escrow.

Collateral - Property used as security for a debt.

Collateral Assignment - An assignment of property for security purposes rather than absolute assignment.

Community Property - Property acquired by a husband and wife while married and not separated, except property acquired by gift, will, or inheritance and certain other items specified by statute. Any other property owned by a husband or wife is separate property.

Comparison Approach - See Market Data Approach.

Compound Interest - Interest computed not only on the principal but also on previously accumulated interest.

Conditional Sale - A contract for the sale of property stating that although delivery is to be made to the buyer, the title is to remain vested in the seller until the conditions of the contract have been fulfilled.

Conditional Sales Contract - See Land Contract.

Consideration - Anything of value given to induce another party to enter into a contract.

Contract - An agreement between two or more parties to do or not to do certain things for the breach of which the law will give a remedy.

Contract for Deed - See Land Contract.

Contract of Sale - See Land Contract.

Conventional Loan - A loan made without government guarantee.

Conveyance - A written instrument that transfers title to or an interest in real property.

Corporation - An artificial person, created by law that has certain powers and duties of a natural person.

Cosigner - A person who signs a note as an additional maker to help another maker secure a loan.

Cost Basis - The aggregate amount an owner pays to acquire an asset plus all capital improvements, if any, less capital losses and depreciation taken.

Credit Report - A report on a credit applicant from a credit reporting service stating creditors' experience with the applicant and frequently containing information or estimates about the applicant's assets, liabilities and character.

Creditor - A person to whom a debt is owed.

Current Value - The value at the time of appraisal.

Debt Financing - The use of borrowed capital to finance the purchase of property.

Debt Service - The sum of money needed each month or year to amortize a loan.

Debtor - A person who owes a debt.

Declining Principal Loan - A loan for which interest is calculated each month, quarter, etc., on the remaining balance of the loan.

Deed - A written instrument transferring title to real property from one person to another.

Deed of Reconveyance - See Reconveyance Deed.

Deed Of Trust - A written instrument transferring bare legal title to real property to a trustee to be held as security for an obligation. Also called a trust deed. The accepted form is presented to the trustee for approval before the execution thereof by the trustor and beneficiary and before recordation. The trustee is therefore duty-bound to perform if he accepts. The automatic form is the most widely used form. It contains a provision whereby the trustee named will accept his duties when the trust deed is properly executed, acknowledged, and recorded and provided he has approved the promissory note and deed of trust. The trustee is not usually aware of the appointment until called on to act in case of default by the trustor.

Default - Failure to fulfill a duty or promise, or to discharge an obligation; omission, or failure to perform an act. In property foreclosure, usually the failure to pay loan installment payments when they become due.

Defeasance Clause - A provision in a mortgage that allows the mortgagor to have his property released from the mortgage when the secured debt is paid.

Deficiency Judgment - A judgment for the amount left unpaid after a property has been sold at a foreclosure sale when the net proceeds are not sufficient to pay off the loan.

Demand Note - A note that is payable on demand of the holder.

Discount - (1) To sell a note for less than the unpaid balance due on it. (2) The dollar difference between the unpaid balance of a note and the price for which a note holder sells the note.

Discount Interest - Interest that is deducted from the principal amount of the loan in advance by the lender on the first day of the loan, hence increasing the lender's yield.

Discount Points - A fee, expressed as a percentage of the loan amount, when making a loan. Points increase the yield.

Dragnet Clause - A clause in a deed of trust that makes it security not only for the present loan but also for any other past or future debts to the beneficiary.

Due-On-Sale Clause - A clause in a note or deed of trust giving the holder the right to declare the entire debt due and payable if the owner sells or contracts to sell the property. Also called a due-on-alienation clause.

Effective Interest Rate - The actual rate of interest the borrower pays in interest for his loan. Also called true interest rate.

Encumbrance - In a legal or technical sense, anything that limits or affects the ownership of property, such as a lien, mortgage, easement or restriction. In the daily language of real estate people, the term usually means a lien.

Endorsement - A signature placed on the back of a note or check to transfer ownership. An endorsement in blank guarantees payment to later holders. An endorsement without recourse, or qualified endorsement, does not guarantee payment to later holders.

Entity - A form of business organization.

Equitable Title - The ownership held by a buyer after he has contracted to buy property but before legal title has been conveyed to him.

Equity in Property - The current market value of a property less the amount of all liens and charges against it.

Equity Loan - Junior (subordinate) loan based on a percentage of the equity.

Equity of Redemption - (1) The right of an owner to redeem his property after he has defaulted on a mortgage. (2) In some states the term is usually applied to the right of an owner to redeem his property for 1 year after judicial foreclosure sale. Also called right of redemption.

Equity Return or Buildup - Dollars paid towards the principal on a loan that reduces the outstanding balance.

Escalation - The raising of some item, such as the interest rate or size of installment payments. The right to escalate the interest rate or size of payment may be given by contract to the lender under specified conditions.

Escalator Clause - A clause providing that an item will be adjusted upward or downward under certain conditions. For example, a note may provide that the interest rate goes up or down as the cost of living index rises or falls.

Escrow: - The deposit of items such as money, deeds, and other instruments by contracting parties with a neutral party, called an escrow holder or escrow agent, to be held until all the terms and conditions of the escrow agreement are fulfilled. Then there is a close of escrow, and the items are delivered to the respective parties entitled to them.

Escrow Officer - An employee of an escrow agent who has the responsibility of handling and closing escrows.

Estoppel Certificate - An instrument executed by a note payer setting forth the status of and the balance due on the promissory note as of the date of the execution of the certificate.

Extension Agreement - An agreement giving additional time in which to pay money or perform some other obligation.

Fee- The fullest estate a person may own in real property. It is the estate almost all owners hold. Also called fee simple.

Fictitious Deed of Trust - A trust deed recorded by a trustee that does not cover an actual transaction. The trustee may then in later deeds of trust refer to the fictitious trust deed and incorporate its terms without repeating them in the part of the trust deed being recorded. This saves recording fees.

Finance Change - The total dollar amount of all charges and interest the lender will make to the borrower over the life of the loan. Includes everything except principal.

Finder's Fee - A fee agreed to be paid to one person, called a finder, who locates another person, such as a buyer or lender, desired by the party promising to pay the fee. The fee is payable when the deal is consummated. In real estate transactions the finder may introduce the parties, but in some states he may not engage in negotiations unless he holds a real estate broker's, mortgage brokers, or a real estate salesman's license.

First Lien - The debt recorded first (earliest in time) such as a first mortgage or first deed of trust. This debt has priority as a lien over all other debts. In cases of foreclosure, the first lien will be satisfied before other liens are paid off.

Foreclosure - The procedure of enforcing a lien by the sale of the property covered by the lien.

Foreclosure Sale - The sale of property in a foreclosure. Most often, it is the sale of the property securing a debt after default in payment.

Free and Clear - Free means a freehold estate, and in this expression it means a fee title. Clear means there are no money encumbrances against the property. Generally used to refer to a property free of mortgage debt.

Future Advance - Money loaned to a borrower after the execution of a trust deed under a clause making the trust deed security for such later advanced. Obligatory future advances are those the lender is required to make under his contract with the borrower. Non obligatory future advances are those the lender is not required to make.

Grace Period - Additional time allowed to perform an act or make a payment before default occurs.

Grant - A term used in deeds of conveyance to indicate a transfer of real property.

Grantee - The party to whom the title to real property is conveyed by deed; the buyer.

Grantor - The party who conveys real property by deed; the seller.

Gross Profit Percentage - Realized gain on the sale or exchange of real property divided by the net sales price of the property. Used to multiply by each year's principal received on a purchase money note to calculate the recognized gain for the year for tax reporting.

Hard Money - (I) Cash loaned: contrasted with soft money, which means credit extended rather than cash. These expressions are often encountered in such a term as hard-money trust deed. (2) Some people use this term to mean a high-interest loan.

Hazard Insurance - Insurance against damage to property from physical hazard, such as fire and windstorm.

Holder in Due Course- A person who takes a negotiable instrument, such as a note or check in good faith for value before it is past due and without notice of any defects when it was negotiated to him. Certain defenses that the maker could have claimed against the original payee, such as payment in full or in part, or certain types of fraud cannot be claimed against a holder in due course.

Hypothecation - Giving real or personal property as security without parting with possession. Installment Contract - See Land Contract.

Installment Note - A promissory note calling for periodic payments.

Installments - Parts of the same debt, payable at successive periods as agreed.

Institutional lender - An institution that makes substantial numbers of real estate loans such as a bank, a savings and loan association or an insurance company.

Instrument - A writing executed as the expression of some contract, act or proceeding; for example, a deed.

Insurable Interest - An interest in property such that damage to the property would cause the owner of the interest a financial loss; for example, the interest of a tenant or the holder of a trust deed.

Interest - (1) Legally, any charge a lender or creditor makes for the use, forbearance or detention of money, no matter how the charge is labeled by the parties. (2) In daily usage, the percentage charged by the lender.

Interest-Only Loan or Note - A loan or note for which the installment payments are 100% interest; thus the payments do not reduce the principal balance of the loan or note.

Interest Rate - The charge made for a loan of money or use of credit, expressed as a percentage of the principal.

Investment-to-value Ratio - When purchasing a note and deed of trust, the amount invested in the note plus the current unpaid balances of all senior loans divided by the current market value or appraised value of the property securing the loans. Investment-to-value ratio is usually expressed as a percentage.

Involuntary Lien - A lien imposed on property without the consent of the owner; for example, real property taxes and judgment liens.

Joint Note - A note in which there are two or more makers who share equal liability on it.

Joint Tenancy - Ownership of property by two or more persons, each of whom has an undivided interest with the right of survivorship.

Joint Venture - A business entity composed of two or more people joined together to conduct a single enterprise for profit. It is treated legally almost like a partnership, but differs from a partnership by having as its objects a single venture instead of a continuing business.

Judgment - A final determination by a court of law. Most often, a judgment is for a sum of money.

Judicial Foreclosure - Foreclosure through court.

Junior Lien - An inferior or subordinate lien. For example, a second deed of trust is a junior to a first trust deed.

Land Contract - A security device used in the sale of real property. The buyer contracts to pay the purchase price in installments. The seller contracts that when the purchase price is paid in full, he will deed the property to the buyer. Until the purchase price is paid in full, the seller keeps legal title. Also called conditional sales contract, contract for deed, contract of sale.

Late Charge - A specified charge added by a creditor under his note or contract when the debtor makes his payment late or after a certain date.

Legal Description - A description of real estate sufficient to allow a competent surveyor to locate the property on the ground.

Level Payments - Payments of equal size.

Lien - A legal right or claim upon a specific property that attaches to the property until the debt is satisfied.

Lien Release - A written agreement by a lien holder releasing the debtor from further obligation.

Limited Partnership - A special type of partnership with one or more general partners who manage the business and are responsible for its debts, and one or more limited partners who take no part in its management and are not responsible for its debts.

Loan-to-Value Ratio - The sum of current unpaid loan balances for all loans against a property divided by the current market value or appraised value of the property securing the loans. Loan-to-value ratio is usually expressed as a percentage.

Lock-in-Clause - A clause in a note, mortgage or trust deed setting a period during which no prepayment is allowed on the loan.

MAI - A designation for a member of the American Institute of appraisers, a part of the National Association of Realtors. The initials stand for Member of American Institute.

Maker - The person who signs a note agreeing to pay it. Also called the payer.

Market Data Approach - An appraisal technique based on sales of comparable properties. Also called comparison approach.

Market Price - The price paid regardless of motives, pressures or intelligence.

Market Value - The highest price, estimated in terms of money, that property would bring if exposed for sale in the open market, allowing a reasonable time to find a buyer who buys with full knowledge of all the uses to which the property is adapted and all the uses for which it is capable of being used.

Mechanic's Lien - A lien given by statute to persons supplying labor, materials or services to improve real property. To perfect the lien, certain notices and recordings are required.

Mortgage - An instrument in writing, duly executed and delivered, that creates a lien upon real estate as security for the payment of a specified debt.

Mortgage Money Market - The source of financing for real estate. It is divided into two parts: The primary mortgage money market consists of all the sources of loans made directly by lenders; the secondary mortgage money market consists of all buyers of existing real estate loans as collateral.

Mortgage Reduction Certificate - An instrument executed by the mortgagee, setting forth the status of and the balance due on the mortgage as of the date of the execution of the instrument.

Mortgagee - The party who lends money and takes a mortgage to secure payment.

Mortgagor - A person who borrows money and gives a mortgage on his or her property as security for the payment of the debt.

Negotiable Instrument - An instrument, such as a check or note, that meets certain legal requirements that allow it to be transferred free of most claims the maker had against previous holders.

Nominal Interest Rate - The rate of interest stated in a note or contract. This may not be the true or effective rate (actual cost) to the borrower.

Non institutional Lender - A lender that is not an institution, such as retirement funds, endowed universities, and private individuals.

Non-judicial Foreclosure - A foreclosure by having property sold to satisfy the debt without going through court.

Notary Public - A person empowered to administer oaths and to attest or certify documents to assure their authenticity.

Note - An instrument in which one party, the maker or payer, promises to pay a definite sum of money to another, the payee, at a fixed or determinable future time or on demand.

Notice of Default - A notice that is recorded and is given to certain people entitled to it stating that a trust deed is in default and that the trust deed holder has chosen to have the property sold. This notice starts the running of a grace period during which the property owner can cure the default by paying up the debt that is past due.

Notice of Trustee's Sale - A notice provided by law requiring the trustee to advertise the property in default in a newspaper of general circulation.

Obligee - A person to whom a legal obligation or duty is owed; for example, the payee of a note.

Obligor - A person who has placed himself under a legal obligation; for example, the maker of a note.

Offset Statement - See Beneficiary Statement.

Open-End Clause - A clause that permits the outstanding balance of the loan to be increased by the borrower under the provisions outlined in the agreement.

Open End Deed of Trust or Mortgage - A trust deed or mortgage that secures not only that original debt but also future advances made after the date of the trust deed or mortgage.

Option - A Contract that gives one party (the optionee) the right to enter into some type of contract upon specified terms with another party (the optionor). Usually, the right to buy the optionor's property or note for a particular price.

Package Deed of Trust or Mortgage - A trust deed or mortgage secured by both real property and personal property.

Partial Reconveyance - A reconveyance that releases a part but not all of a tract from the lien of a trust deed or mortgage.

Partial Release Clause - A provision in a trust deed, mortgage or land contract that permits the borrower or buyer to secure the release of part of the property by complying with certain terms, such as the payment of a certain sum of money.

Partnership - A voluntary association of two or more persons to carry on business for profit.

Payee - A person to whom a note states it is payable.

Payer - A person who signs a note agreeing to pay it. Also called a maker.

Point -1 % of the principal amount of a loan. A lender often charges points when a loan is made, renewed or assumed, to raise the yield on the loan.

Power -of-Sale Clause - A clause in trust deeds and in some mortgages giving the trustee or mortgagee the right to sell the property that is security for the loan at public sale, without court procedure, if the debtor defaults.

Preliminary Title Insurance Report - A report by a title insurance company showing the condition of title to a property including liens, restrictions, etc.

Prepayment - To pay off all or part of a debt before it is due.

Prepayment Clause - A provision in a note or deed of trust allowing the borrower to pay off all or part of the principal before it is due, with or without a prepayment penalty.

Prepayment Penalty - A charge provided in a note or deed of trust for the privilege of paying all or part of the debt before it is due.

Primary Financing - The loan which has first priority; the loan which has its security instrument recorded first.

Primary Mortgage Money Market - See Mortgage Money Market.

Principal - The capital amount of a loan, not including interest. The principal portion of an installment payment on a loan reduces the outstanding balance of the loan by the amount of the principal payment.

Principal Plus Interest Loan - A loan for which the borrower makes a fixed principal payment each period and pays, in addition, interest on the unpaid principal amount of the loan.

Promissory Note - See Note.

Purchase Money Deed of Trust or Mortgage - A trust deed or mortgage given to secure all or part of the purchase price of real estate.

Quitclaim Deed - A deed that conveys simply the grantor's rights or interest in real estate; generally considered inadequate except when interests are being passed from one spouse to the other.

Rate of Return - See Yield Rate.

Realized Gain - Total profit on the sale or exchange of real property. Computed as net sales price less cost basis.

Real Property - Land and things attached to the land, such as buildings and other appurtenances.

Recognized Gain - The amount of the realized gain on the sale or exchange of real property reportable in a given year on tax returns.

Reconveyance Deed - A deed from a trustee under a trust deed conveying legal title back to the property owner to release the lien of the trust deed. Also called a deed of reconveyance.

Recordation - The recording of an instrument in the county recorder's office to give constructive notice of it.

Recourse - The right to claim against a prior owner of a property or note.

Redemption - (1) The correcting of a default under a trust deed or mortgage by paying the entire indebtedness plus foreclosure costs. (2) The reacquiring (buying back) of property sold at a judicial foreclosure sale by paying the amount for which it was sold plus certain other items specified by statute. See also Equity of Redemption.

Refinance - To obtain new financing to pay off an existing loan.

Reinstatement - The curing of a default under a trust deed or mortgage by paying up the amount past due. Reinstatement restores the loan to the status it had before the default.

Release Clause - A provision in a blanket mortgage or trust deed allowing the owner of the properties to secure the release of properties upon certain terms, usually the payment of a certain sum of money.

Release of Liability - A letter or other form of release that relieves a debtor of any further responsibility on his debt or other obligation.

Release of Mortgage - A written instrument releasing the lien of a mortgage on real property. See also Certificate of Discharge.

Request for Reconveyance - An instrument executed by a trust deed holder directing the trustee to convey legal title to the property involved back to the owner. Most often, a form for this request is printed on the back of the trust deed so that the creditor may execute it when the debt is satisfied. Nevertheless, it may also be a separate instrument.

Rescind - To cancel a contract or other transaction and restore to each what he had given under it.

Rescission - (I) The act of rescinding. (2) A legal action to rescind a contract or other transaction.

Restriction - A limitation upon the use of property that is specified in the title deed.

Return - See Yield.

Right of Redemption - See Equity of Redemption.

Right of Survivorship - Right of the surviving joint owner to succeed to the interest of the deceased joint owner.

Satisfaction - Performance of the terms of a contract, usually by payment in full of an obligation.

Satisfied - Paid or performed in full.

Second Loan - A loan secured by a second deed of trust or mortgage.

Secondary Mortgage Money Market - See Mortgage Money Market.

Secured Party - The person for whose benefit security is given.

Set-Off - A claim a debtor is entitled to make against a creditor that reduces or eliminates the amount the debtor owes the creditor.

Simple Interest - Interest computed on the unpaid principal amount of the loan without provisions for additional interest to be paid on interest.

Soft Money - Credit extended as opposed to cash (hard money). Also, see Purchase Money Deed of Trust or Mortgage.

Straight Note - A promissory note with the principal payable in one lump sum instead of in installments.

Stipulations - The terms within a written contract.

Subordination - The act of making an existing loan secondary or junior to another lien or loan.

Subordination Agreement - A contract by which the holder of a prior lien makes it junior or inferior to another lien.

Substitution of Mortgagor - An agreement in which the lender on a loan being assumed by buyer agrees to relieve the original borrower of liability.

Substitution of Trustee -An instrument that the beneficiary under a trust deed executes and records to substitute a new trustee for an earlier one.

Tenancy in Common - An ownership of real property by two or more persons, each of whom has an undivided interest, without right of survivorship.

Term - A provision of a loan or contract that specifies the length of time the contract is to run.

Title - Evidence of the ownership of real property.

Title Company - Firm examining title to real property and/or issuing title insurance.

Title Defect - Unresolved claim against the ownership of property that prevents presentation of a marketable title. Such claims may arise from failure of the owner's spouse, or former part owner, to sign a deed, current liens against the property, or an interruption in the title records of a property.

Title Insurance - Insurance that protects against loss because of faulty title.

Title Report - Document indicating the current state of the title, such as easements, covenants, liens and any other defects. The title report does not describe the chain of title. See also Abstract of Title.

Title Search -An examination of the public records to determine ownership and encumbrances affecting real property.

Trust Deed - See Deed of Trust.

Trustee - A person who holds bare legal title to real or personal property for the benefit of another person. A trustee is one of the parties in a trust deed.

Trustee's Deed - A deed issued to the successful bidder at a trustee's sale. A trustee's deed conveys title to the purchaser free and clear, but subject to all senior liens.

Trustor – A person who conveys property to a trustee. In a trust deed the trustor is the borrower or debtor.

Undivided Interest – Ownership of real estate by joint tenants or tenants in common under the same title.

Unsecured – Without security.

Usury - The charging of more interest than is allowed by law.

Valid - Having force, or binding force; legally sufficient and authorized by law.

Valuation - Estimated worth or price. The act of valuing by appraisal.

Vendee - A buyer.

Vendee's Lien - A lien against real property under a land contract to secure a deposit paid by a purchaser

Vendor - A seller.

Void - (1) Having no legal effect; null. (2) To have an instrument transaction declared void.

Voidable - That which is capable of being adjudged void, but is not void unless action is taken to make it so.

Voluntary Lien – A lien intentionally put on real property by the owner.

Waiver - The renunciation, abandonment or surrender of some claim, right or privilege.

Warranty Deed - A conveyance of real property in which the grantor guarantees the title to the grantee.

Without Recourse - Words used endorsing a note to denote that the future holder is not to look to the endorser in case of non-payment.

Wrap-Around Contract of Sale, Mortgage or Trust Deed - A land contract, mortgage, or trust deed that works like this: The debtor owns or buys property with a first deed of trust seller on it. A seller or second lender takes a second deed of trust or second mortgage or a land contract for an amount that includes not only the amount owed to this second party but also the amount of the first trust deed. The owner makes one monthly payment to this second party. Out of it the second party makes the payment on the first trust deed and keeps the rest as his payment. Also called all-inclusive contract of sale, mortgage or trust deed.

Yield - Interest earned by the lender on the money loaned. Also called return.

Yield Rate - Yield expressed as a percentage of the total investment. Also called rate of return.

Illustrations

Deposit Receipt and Sales Purchase Contract

Received from _____

_____

the buyer, the sum of _____

dollars ($_____) to be held in escrow by

_____

Escrow Agent, as a deposit on account of the purchase price of the following described

property:

_____

_____

_____

_____

_____

_____

_____

_____

Purchase Price: $_____Dollars

($_____)

Terms and conditions of sale:

PURCHASE PRICE SHALL BE PAID AS FOLLOWS:

1. Purchaser shall pay $_____ cash at closing of which the deposit is a
    part thereof, and

2. Purchaser shall take subject to an existing mortgage in favor of _____, with
    an approximate principal balance of $_____ with payments thereon in the
    amount of $_____ per month which includes interest at the annual rate of
    _____%, and

3. Purchaser shall execute in favor of and deliver to seller a note in the principal amount of (Example) $12,000.00 that shall call for repayment of principal together with interest as per the following eight year schedule:

Example:

During note year	Principal repayment	Monthly payments
One	$1,500.00	$131.87
Two	1,500.00	144.37
Three	1,500.00	156.87
Four	1,500.00	169.37
Five	1,500.00	181.87
Six	1,500.00	194.37
Seven	1,500.00	206.87
Eight	1,500.00	219.37

The above schedule includes 10% simple interest per annum. The note shall be secured be a mortgage against the subject property, which said property shall be the exclusive security for the repayment of the debt without personal liability on the part of the Purchaser/maker.

The broker in this transaction is _____

The seller agrees to sell and the buyer agrees to buy the above described property for the price and on the terms herein set forth, including the terms and conditions set forth on the reverse side on this contract. Time is of the essence of this contract and the terms of this contract shall be binding upon both parties, the seller and the buyer, their heirs, personal representatives, successors and assigns.

Upon execution by both the Buyer and Seller, this Deposit Receipt shall become a Real Estate Sale/Purchase Contract incorporating all terms on the reverse except as otherwise specifically modified on the face hereof. READ THIS CONTRACT FULLY ON THE FRONT AND REVERSE SIDES PRIOR TO SIGNATURE.

Signed, sealed and delivered in the presence of: _____

Witnesses to Buyer: Date: _____

_____

_____

Buyer: _____   Date: _____

_____

_____

Promissory Note

$_____ \quad _____(Place)_____ \quad \_\_\_\_(Date)_____ \quad pay to the order of _____the principal sum of _____dollars ($_____ _____) together with interest thereon from this date at the rate of_____ percent per annum until maturity. The said principal and interest being payable at _____, or at such other place as the holder hereof may designate in writing. The said principal and interest being payable as follows:

(Here include the specific terms of the note.)

This note may be prepaid in whole or in part at any time without penalty

This note is secured by a mortgage of even date herewith and is to be construed and enforced according to the laws of the State of _____. Upon the makers' failure to pay any sum required to be paid by the terms of this note or the securing mortgage, promptly when they severally become, or upon the breach of any stipulation, agreement or covenant of this note or of the securing mortgage, the entire sum of principal and interest remaining unpaid shall, at the option of the holder hereof, become immediately due and payable. Failure to exercise said option shall not constitute a waiver of the right to exercise the same at any subsequent time.

This note, including any installment payment of principal and/or interest, shall bear interest at the rate of _____% per annum from the respective maturity dates thereof until paid.

Each maker and endorser agrees, jointly and severally, to pay all cost of collection, including a reasonable attorney's fee, if this note, including any installment payment, is not paid promptly when due, and the same is given to any attorney for collection, whether suit be brought or not.

Each maker and endorser severally waives demand, protest, and notice of maturity, non-payment, or protest and notice of maturity, non-payment or protest and all other requirements necessary to hold each of them liable as makers and endorsers

_____(Seal)

_____(Seal)

Mortgage

Short Form

THIS INDENTURE, made this _____day of _____, A.D. 20_____,
BETWEEN _____hereinafter called the
Mortgagor, and _____hereinafter called the
Mortgagee,

WITNESSETH, that the said Mortgagor, for and in consideration of the sum of One
Dollar ($1.00), to _____ in hand paid by the said Mortgagee, the
receipt whereof is hereby acknowledged, granted, bargained and sold to the said Mortgagee,
_____heirs and assigns forever, the
following described land situate, lying, and being in the County of_____, State of
_____, to wit (deed description): _____   and the said
Mortgagor do hereby fully warrant the title to said land, and will defend the same against the
lawful claims of all persons whomsoever.

PROVIDED ALWAYS, that if said Mortgagor, _____ heirs, legal
representatives or assigns shall pay unto the said Mortgagee, _____ legal
representatives or assigns, certain promissory note dated the _____day of _____,
A.D. 20_____, for the sum of _____dollars,   payable
_____   with   interest   at   _____   percent   from
_____ signed by _____ and shall
perform, comply with and abide by each this mortgage, and shall pay all taxes which may accrue
on said land and all costs and expenses said Mortgagee may be put to in collecting said promissory note by foreclosure of this mortgage or otherwise, including a reasonable attorney's fee,
then this mortgage and the estate hereby created shall cease and be null and void.

IN   WITNESS   WHEREOF,   the   said   Mortgagor   hereunto   set
_____hand and seal _____the day and year first
above written.

Signed, sealed, and delivered in presence of us:

(_____)   _____(SEAL)

(_____)   _____(SEAL

Sample Contract Clauses

The clauses on the following pages are included to give the reader insight into the many variations and areas of negotiation in a purchase contract. Any one of the clauses can be expanded upon. Use this section to provoke thought of new angles and protective considerations for your purchase agreements.

STRAIGHT NOTE (ONE PAYMENT)

Purchaser to execute in favor of the seller a straight Promissory Note due in full on
_____ together with _____% interest per annum simple.

INTEREST STATED AS DOLLARS

together with $_____ interest

QUARTERLY PAYMENTS (INTEREST ONLY WITH BALLOON)

Purchaser shall execute and deliver to the seller a note in the amount of
$_____ (secured by a mortgage against the property) calling for quarterly
interest payments of _____ with the full principal balance due on

_____.

MONTHLY PAYMENTS (AMORTIZED)

Purchaser to execute a note secured by a _____ mortgage on the property, in
favor of the seller, in the principal amount of $_____ payable at
$_____ per _____, or more, including interest at
_____% per annum, until paid.

MONTHLY PAYMENTS SECURED BY WRAPAROUND PAYMENTS MADE TO A SERVICING COMPANY

Purchaser to execute a note, in favor of the seller in the principal amount of $_____,
to be payable at _____ per_____ with interest at the rate of
_____ % per annum. Said note shall be secured by a WRAPAROUND mortgage
against the property. Said wraparound mortgage shall call for the maker of the note to make their
payments to:

_____

_____

as collection agent (Herein known as Collection Agent) for the _____.
The Collection Agent shall upon receipt of the purchaser's payment disburse to and pay all underlying obligations in existence at time of closing, with the balance of any such payment to be disbursed to the seller. The cost of such collection service shall be borne by the

_____.

NOTE CREATED AND SOLD

Purchaser shall execute a note in favor of the seller in the principal amount of $_____ payable at $ _____ per _____, together with _____ interest per annum. The note shall be secured by a mortgage on the property. The note and mortgage shall be sold to an investor at closing for $_____

MORATORIUM ON PAYMENTS

The note executed by the purchaser shall call for a moratorium as to payments and interest, for a period of _____, at which time payments shall commence in the amount of $_____ payable _____ together with interest in the amount of _____% per annum until paid.

STUTTER CLAUSE

The maker of the note reserves the right to miss one such period payment per loan year and failure to make such periodic payment shall not be a default of the said note.

FIRST REFUSAL TO PURCHASE NOTE

The maker of this note reserves the right of first refusal if the note is ever offered for sale and or trade, and expressly reserves the right to match any offer acceptable to the holder of the note.

SUBORDINATION CLAUSE

The seller agrees to subordinate this note and mortgage to any new financing the purchaser might secure with the property at some time in the future. Furthermore the seller agrees to execute any documentation necessary to effect such subordination.

SUBSTITUTION OF COLLATERAL

The purchaser reserves the right to substitute other collateral for the purchase money note, from time to time. The seller herein agrees to execute whatever documents that are necessary to effect said substitution.

EXCULPATORY CLAUSE

The property shall be the sole security for the note, and there is no personal liability on the part of the maker.

EXTENDING DUE DATE

The maker reserves the right to extend the due date of the note for an additional year with the payment of $_____ to the holder of the note thirty (30) days prior to the due date.

SUBJECT TO PARTNER (with time limit)

This agreement is subject to an inspection of the property by the purchaser's partner, or his assigns, within five (5) business days of the seller's acceptance of this agreement.

SUBJECT TO LEASES

This agreement is subject to the purchaser inspecting and accepting all leases and or rental agreements at or prior to closing.

SUBJECT TO ATTORNEY

This agreement is subject to the inspection and approval of the _____'s attorney within five (5) business days of the _____.

SUBJECT TO FINANCING

This agreement is subject to the purchaser acquiring suitable financing within _____ days from the signing of this agreement by both parties.

SUBJECT TO FINDING A TENANT

This agreement is subject to and closing shall not occur before the purchaser is able to secure a tenant that is acceptable to the purchaser, and at a rental rate of $_____ per _____, or at such other rental rate that might be acceptable to the **purchaser.**

RECORDING A MEMORANDUM

By mutual agreement a short form of this agreement shall be signed and acknowledged by all parties to this agreement and recorded in the Public Records of_____ County, State of _____.

TAKING SUBJECT TO EXISTING LOAN

The purchaser shall take the property subject to the existing first mortgage held in favor of _____ without any escalation of interest, or additional cost on the part of the purchaser.

ESCROW/IMPOUND ACCOUNTS

The mortgage escrow account shall be transferred to the purchaser at closing, without additional cost to the purchaser, as a part of the purchase price. Any deficiencies in said account shall be paid by the seller at closing.

PAYMENT OF PROPERTY TAXES

The seller herein agrees to pay property taxes for the year of the sale.

LOAN BALANCE DISCREPANCY

In the event there is any discrepancy in the balance of any underlying existing mortgage as stated in the contract, any difference shall be adjusted in the sales price and not in the down payment. In no event though shall the purchase price exceed $_____ nor the down payment exceed $_____. The seller warrants that all existing mortgages shall be current at time of closing.

SELLER TO PAY CLOSING COSTS

The purchaser shall pay his own attorney's fees, and fees for advance payments for hazard insurance, the seller shall pay the remaining closing cost.

EXTENSION OF CLOSING

The payment of the earnest money deposit herein is consideration for the purchaser to have the option of extending the closing _____ days.

SELLER TO PROVIDE TITLE INSURANCE

The seller shall deliver, at his own expense, to the purchaser a title insurance policy with a face amount of $_____ five (5) days prior to closing for the purchaser's examination and approval.

SELLER TO PROVIDE A SURVEY

The seller shall deliver at its own expense a certified survey completed within the last three (3) months, to the purchaser, five (5) days prior to closing.

LIQUIDATED DAMAGES CLAUSE

The _____ Dollar ($_____) earnest money deposit shall be retained by the seller as total liquidated damages in the event that the buyer defaults on the performance of this agreement.

BUYER TO PAY SELLER'S BROKERAGE FEE

The purchaser reserves the right to pay the seller's real estate brokerage fees, and to receive credit for same against the _____.

SELLER WARRANTS IMPROVEMENTS

The seller warrants that the grounds and improvements will be maintained, that the roof and facia are water tight and in good repair, and all appliances, heating, air conditioning, plumbing, sewer or septic, and electrical systems shall be in good working order at close of escrow. The seller agrees to permit the inspection thereof by agents of the purchaser, prior to close of escrow, and to pay for any repairs called for by said inspections. The seller agrees to use licensed persons to make said repairs. The purchaser reserves the right of accepting the cash equivalent in lieu of the repairs.

Index

BOOKS, COURSES

and

SEMINARS

By

E. Wright Davis

Mega Mortgages

4-Day DVD Seminar conducted by E. Wright Davis

Mega Mortgages is a comprehensive course on the Cash-Flow Industry. This four-day DVD course will take the student from grammar school to graduate school in cash flow investing.

In this course, you will learn:

√ The basics of discounted notes and mortgages.

√ How the principles of the time value of money will make you wealthy.

√ How to find, buy, and sell notes for big profits.

√ How to buy real estate at a discount with no money down, a positive cash flow and put money in your pocket at closing.

√ How to pay off your house in 5 years without having to make a house payment.

√ How to receive 31+% yield on notes using none of your own money.

√ How to buy notes with no money down.

√ How to get free notes without foreclosures short sales or hard money loans.

√ How to get a free $80,000 IRA.

√ How to buy a business with notes.

√ How to get a free house.

√ Eliminate the risks.

√ How to use the financial calculator.

√ Partial purchases.

√ Note possibilities.

√ Marketing.

√ The nuts, bolts and paperwork.

√ Nitch markets.

√ The law and the discount paper business.

With this course you will receive:

√ DVD copies of a live 4-day presentation by E. Wright Davis of *Mega Mortgages, Calculator Power!* and *How To Crack the Mortgage Code.*

√ Software which shows how to utilize the 19 techniques contained in *How To Crack the Mortgage Code* without having to use a financial calculator.

√ *How to Crack The Mortgage Code*…a complete manual containing and forms… a $69 value.

√ *Mega Mortgages*… a complete manual containing pages, forms, and a DVD live presentation… a $1,295 value.

√ *Getting Started in Creative Real Estates Investing*… this manual contains forms and examples of typical contract clauses….a $39 value.

√ *Calculator Power!* A complete 210 page manual. A simple hands on guide to using a financial calculator– a $249 value.

If the above items were to be purchased separately, the cost would be $1,652.

The cost for this 4-day seminar <u>including all of the items above</u>:

$695… a savings of $957

How to Crack the Mortgage Code

The 19 Greatest Ways To Pay Off Your Mortgage Fast

by E. Wright Davis

In this Course Package, you will receive:

1. A complete workbook/manual with forms

2. A 2-hour DVD live presentation on how to utilize the 19 techniques

You will learn:

√ How to save hundreds of thousands of dollars in unnecessary interest payments.

√ How to reduce the payoff period of a mortgage from 30 years to 5-10 years.

√ How to stop foreclosures cold.

√ The 8 mortgage myths.

√ The secrets behind the time value of money principles.

√ How to create a cash flow machine from real estate.

Cost: $69 (plus shipping and handling)

Calculator Power
By Jon Richards and David Roberts
Course by E. Wright Davis
(Included as a BONUS in the seminar package)

This is the most comprehensive real estate finance course ever.

This page manual and the accompanying FREE DVD's will give you all the hands on step-by-step instruction on every aspect of the operation of the financial calculator you will ever need.

This is a full 8-hour course with comprehensive easy to understand instructions.

With this course, you will learn how to:

√ Structure offers to buy real estate.

√ Structure real estate financing utilizing the concepts of the time value of money.

√ A step-by-step approach to calculating payments on a loan.

√ Calculate the remaining balance due on a mortgage.

√ Calculate balloon payments

√ Calculate time value of money concepts.

√ Calculate the present value of streams of real estate income.

√ Calculate discount real estate income to present value

√ Make offers that will insure more closing utilizing these concepts.

Cost: $249 Plus shipping and handling.

To Place Your Book Order

On the internet or by phone:

Information for ordering E. Wright Davis's books on the internet or by phone using a credit card or PayPal can be found at:

www.ewrightdavis.com

Viewing Live Streaming Seminars & Webinars via the internet

To view live streaming seminars and/or webinars via the internet, complete instructions to sign up with details regarding dates, times and registration fees can be found at:

www.ewrightdavis.com

Attending E. Wright Davis's Live Seminars in person:

To attend one of E. Wright Davis's live seminars in person, complete details regarding location, dates, times and registration fees can be found at:

www.ewrightdavis.com

www.ingramcontent.com/pod-product-compliance
Lightning Source LLC
Chambersburg PA
CBHW071940220326
41599CB00033BA/6556